VEDDER AHEAD:

modern stories from the west coast of America

Stuart Newton

4/2016

Best wishes
SN ***

emp3 books

www.emp3books.com

This book is a work of fiction. The names, characters and incidents in this book are the work of the author's imagination. Any resemblances to any persons living or dead or any locations or scenarios are purely coincidental.

Published in August 2012 by emp3books,
Norwood House, Elvetham Road, Fleet, GU51 4HL

©Stuart Newton

The author asserts the moral right to be identified as the author of this work

ISBN-13: 978-1-907140-63-1

The cover photo is the Vedder River at Chilliwack which flows into the Fraser River, in BC Canada, taken in late September

www.emp3books.com

CONTENTS

Dedication: this book is for David Kennedy, Laurence Braybrook and Jack Derringer – real American men, out-an-about in well favored country

iii

FOREWORD

These stories take place on the West Coast (US and Canada) in the 1960's/70's; where I lived and worked for many years. They are in an arbitrary order, to create suspense and direct the reader away from obvious connections; to break-up the narrative line and bring new moods/themes to the fore. There was a multitude of things going-on along this coast with many different kinds of people; making for an attractive destination and some fascinating accounts -- all the way from mountain skylines in Yosemite Park, deserts in the south and timber forests further north. In between were goldfields and panhandlers, dreamers and rednecks; coming together to make a brave new kind of world. This coast is a very big territory; stretching all the way from Mexico further south, right up to the Yukon snows – small towns and famed cities, farming and colleges, work and travel, with hopes and dreams. I once joined a construction crew on the Peace River, together with native Indians/native sons; years later tended a service station, in middle California, with local lads from the Junior college.

Before all that, back in England, I chanced to read about Nick Adams (Ernest Hemingway) and his adventures in the mid-west of America. His character was lowly and young; exploring a native country very much on his own and learning about himself, in a way I found compelling and instructive. Essentially, the scenes were rural and homegrown; with a new kind of 'voice' that was natural and strong. I soon found myself in similar territory when first moving to Canada, then going onto California; to find the renown vineyards and beach playgrounds, the artists and students, science and entertainment -- a wonderful mix of people and locations. But I was not in a position to write about this untill decades later. Eventually, after visiting Ketchum in Idaho (2010), where Hemingway lived his last years; I very much wanted to complete this book. It was a long road-trip from Vancouver (thousands of miles), up into the Rocky Mountains, then straight south towards a small mining town made-over into a vacation resort. Ketchum cemetery remains in the centre of town, where two well-appointed gravestones lie flat under two small pine trees, inviting visitors and fans to see the end of something.

It was the red soil in California, which first caught my attention, as a young boy in England. I saw this deep red earth in 'The Red Pony', a Hollywood movie from Steinbeck's short novel and again with Rock Hudson in 'This Earth is Mine', where native sons fought over their vineyards. The land seemed to be very fertile, full of promise and the people full of passion, more than I had known before. By the time I lived in Santa Cruz on the coast, Steinbeck and Saroyan were already familiar to me, their endearing characters forming a full background to my own adventures. Raymond Chandler came to me much later, after leaving Canada for London (UK); when I read about a tough corner of the US, with troubled people and difficult situations. But his gritty attitude (from Los Angeles) helped my writing of this book, more especially with the dialogue. Of course America/Canada has moved-on a lot, from the days of Nick Adams (or Philip Marlowe). Still, I looked forward to exploring the west coast for myself; developing my new taste for country life, small towns and young men out working in basic employment.

The vast conifer forests of Canada continue to dominate the landscapes and the livelihood for folk upon them. Native Indians still reside in large numbers, as consolidated communities; trying to direct their lives in the old ways, inspite of modern changes. The population further south has greatly increased, developed -- compared to scattered settlements in the north. But the west coast is always open to newcomers with their hopes and dreams, yearnings and wanderings; as good opportunity to discover things about yourself and life itself -- warm and inviting, big and roomy.

*   *   *

At the beginning of each story is a short vignette, set forth as a kind of 'taster', to whet the appetite for what follows. Hemingway used this same format in 'In our Time' to good effect and I wanted to follow this form; because these intros inform the stories or make for a lively contrast. There is no direct connection between the two sections; but themes may connect, moods and situations follow on or flow into each other...

*   *   *

I have deliberately not identified any place or any persons in the text. Though some of these people/places may be recognized, because they are meant to be real and alive -- yet never intending to hurt, embarrass or offend anyone or anyplace with writing these pages. This book is basically a work of fiction, meant for pleasure and reflection.

PRELUDE

One came from the street and the other person was already standing on the proverbial corner, looking both ways. When the two figures converged, they went inside a café to sit.

"Well, are we ready"?

"Just deliver these keys and sign some papers" he said.

"You got the tickets" she asked?

"Yes, I got two seats together".

The dawn was coming, coming fast above the quiet dark; above tired people, confused people, every kind of disquiet. He could see this all the time they spoke, specially when she spoke and glanced about, above the items in front, on the table between them; because it was getting very close.

"Okay, let's go" --

"Got enough money for us"?

The man rose to a good height, adjusted his pants, his belt and started to move smoothly to the door, the street, his getaway car at the kerb. The woman also stood and bent over with lank hair; she was rumpled and frowning, but could not think of anything more than a nod and then fell into step with him. They went out quickly, together, as if not to be noticed.

For a while the man was cruising the parking lot like a mean cop, but he was only looking for an empty space, a place to leave his trusty wheels. Their meeting was in ten minutes and he sensed her walking at an unhappy pace, as if something was not right. But no more talk would work, it was too late. She had a lot to worry over and needed a man to take-up the slack and listen. He was strangely unsmiling and watchful, as if withholding a secret.

"Don't worry, this won't take long".

"Okay, fine". But it did, take a long time; to make them restless and strained, exposed and defenseless. Though from a distance they

ix

looked like any regular couple, like everyone else, out very early in the morning or very late from the night. Either way, love and friendship are always difficult: needing luck and strength or clever plans.

They could be brother and sister, man-an-wife, or newly met – because California was oblique and slanted high to the modern way; relationships and feelings or yearnings and anxieties, could be misleading and unhelpful, stretched to the limit. Both men and women had to struggle within the favourable climate; with abundance and choice serving as both opportunity and warning. Sometimes danger and risk, or just plain uncertainty, could really help people; hardship and hurt might set them straight, to give them a chance at escape and to be real.

"Are you sure about this" she asked, when they returned to the parked vehicle?

"It's not a coincidence" as he held up the tickets "someone is watching" --

CHAPTER ONE

The girl was wearing a woollen smock, which flowed round her knees when she smiled and talked to her escort, a young man from unknown parts. It was sunny that day, like a promise of early summer coming and warm enough for them to amble along a favourite shoreline; where sand-grass grew between flinty rocks and the ocean sent gentle waves across the beach. They covered a lot of ground that morning, because he had been away, working with a survey crew further north and out of touch. The girl was glad to talk and make a new start, he trying to keep-up at her side, when she suddenly started to limp –

"What's wrong" he said?

"Look, a butterfly, on my skirt" and she pointed to a pair of wings adorned with a black-an-gold pattern, clinging onto the hem in front. It was a monarch butterfly and they were known to travel through California, going south every year, just like this one. By now the girl was trying to befriend the creature, to stay with her long as possible; while she began to lower her voice, climbing over the rocks very carefully. The young man also tried to help, by becoming silent and watchful.

"It's a sign of good luck" she said, looking down at the fluttering wings attached to her, with a lot of pride and patience --

"I hope so" he replied.

BICYCLE FRIENDS

Rudolph Borah was a young man without any college or immediate family support; but he left home in the Mid-West to try his luck on the West Coast, to find a job and place to stay. Now he wanted wheels to get around the town, even though it was very small and someone promised help with this. Rudi had a lot of people to

1

keep-up with that year and they were mostly older, so had to defer to them and stand to order when visiting. One such man had a nice place near the center of town; a long-time graduate student, often moody and pedantic after too many hours at his books.

"I got a bicycle for you" the student said "and you like mine, don't you! So I got to thinking" --

"Yeah, terrific, great idea; where is it"?

"Behind the Palomar Club, down Pacific Avenue. You know the place"?

"Yep, think I remember. At the far end towards the ocean; right"?

"Yes, round the back; been there two weeks and no one claiming it. A blue, full-size man's cycle, no one else wants". He was working at his reading texts again, but enjoyed getting Rudi charged up with an idea of possession and promise. It was a quick strike for college liberals and conservation ideas. After another ten minutes attendance in the apartment rooms Rudi left, determined to visit the club next day, before going to his work place in the afternoon.

"Thanks-a-lot"!

"Just wanna do you a favour; that's all"!

But Rudi knew it would make a reliance upon the student, like had happened before; to become a debt of gratitude not easily repayable. He already knew how this friend liked involving him in obligations and courtesies not fully understood, because the West Coast was not his domain; he still the green ole-country stick, a newly made-over resident. California was always the Great Bear Republic, proud and independent, ready to play and tease any visitor from out of state.

Next day he got to the drinking club at opening time and put a clever line to the bar-man, because it was a real prize for him. "I lost my bike", claimed Rudi. "Have yuh seen it; left about two weeks ago"? Because Rudi could not find it out back, like the student said he would.

"What you after; a bike? Yeah I seen it. Blue, yuh said"?

"Yep, that's the one", said Rudi not to waste his time and to make it easy for them.

2

"Yeah, still outside, round to the left. Check down the concrete steps; I saw it today".

"Thanks" – he called out over his shoulder.

Sure enough Rudi found it down narrow steps leading to a storage basement. Twelve steps to the bottom, he saw it lying like a crumpled child chased from home. Rudi descended the steep stairs, taking the thing to heart from first sight; to become his first bicycle since school days. He picked it up by both wheels and lifted to the yard above, where he saw the pedal-chain misplaced and rear wheel dislodged from the frame; but nothing too serious to fix. He was glad to take a broken bike home, to find a place for it and do the necessary repairs.

Back at his garage rooms Rudi let a neighbour see the damage, to help him re-oil the moving parts and borrow his hand tools. Lots of quick ideas went between them that morning, to assist and mend; then only left for him to inflate the tires at the corner gas station and ride away. His old Chevy auto sat on the dirt space behind a row of shrubbery for the next week, untouched and unnoticed for a change, while Rudi went back-an-forth into town with the bike at every opportunity.

By Friday Rudi sat in a popular diner, because he could afford steak-an-potato after a full week at work; six days on the line, ten hour shifts heaving crates of farm produce round the cannery sheds. It was a good grill, a clean and well-lit place and he ate slow so as to think how it tasted, how it smelled; to eat in a quiet corner at evening. He looked across the tables to see no one of any import, no work mates from his job site, because he did not want that. But he did see a young lady; a striking girl with strands of hair dark as a crow cutting across her cheek. When she saw him, she also stood up, as time for her to leave and be somewhere else. He was hoping it would be to meet someone worthwhile. Rudi continued slicing into the medium beef and chopped at the potato like he didn't care; but he was hungry, happy and hungry after ten hours of honest labour.

"Can I sit here", she said? A girl loosened her coat in front of the

3

young man and sat across from him. She talked some more, like it was a regular night when young people met in cafes for refreshment, then go off with each other for the night.

"Let's walk out Rudi, let's go", she said.

"Not finished yet".

But something warmed up between them, as she remained seated and Rudi kept dealing with the potato and the slippery beans. She tried to watch him fairly, without fear or favour, waiting and listening.

"I need coffee now, before I go anywhere" said Rudi.

"You want some"?

"No".

"You must have the coffee with me, come on".

By the time they stepped down Front Street Rudi was full and satisfied, the girl keeping-up at his elbow, going out together into the open darkness of a small town. Sea breezes cease to blow at dusk on the coast and Rudi discerned his breathing in the salty evening air, the same as last night, to distract his attention. The girl was twenty-something and attractive; one of the group Rudi went round with. She talked about their gang, the recent goings on and pulled up her sleeves to show nut-brown arms. Rudi could also see strong limbs of a woman in best health. He always liked her full appeal and maintained an equal pace down the sidewalk.

"David gave it me. Damn him", she said!

"How is he"?

"Now I'm on shots and medication this month".

"And Dave too"?

"I don't like penicillin stuff".

By this time they went over four cross-sections; even waiting for a green light when at ten-pm no one was about. As they stood by a red light the girl stretched her arms to her shoulders in a fine gesture of womanly confidence and possible intimacy, with only Rudi in benefit. Her light skirt was helping to display fine physique, a good straight torso. Rudi had seen all this in the diner and before that, with

4

sessions of the gang in their cafe-bar up Pacific Avenue. Now at night he wanted to see something else -- to see how the darkness was non-threatening in California and where the empty pavement welcomed night walkers; how Rudi felt cool air on his red neck, sore hands and what he thought about this town after his nine months stay. Rudi was considerate like that and he also appreciated a woman who appealed to basic instincts and appealed to other men.

But the warmth between them from the eating house was running out, as they got to the intersection of Front Street and Panorama, at a long red light in front of four traffic lanes. The girl pressed up against Rudi with one arm at his waist, a hand on his chest.

"Let's go home", she said.

"Why's that"?

"Let's go and make love. I haven't done it for weeks because David is with Sharon. You know what I mean".

"We thought he was -- with her, I mean. But why you talking like this and why me"?

She held on a bit longer with the rhetoric, as it began, but not in concert with her grasping his abdomen again. Rudi allowed the pleading to run on, to defuse the frontal assault, as the girl came out with her purpose along with her consent.

"I can't", Rudi said calmly and evenly as he could, when he relaxed on a wider stance. The girl reversed, then went for his waist again, to make a case for basic sexuality; a simple exchange of freedom and affection. When her hands released an unmoved body, Rudi claimed fear, a fear of sexual disease. Yet the girl was not sympathetic; she was more insistent and went on to hint at ridicule and her being confounded.

"I don't want what you got" he added, "I heard what it's like". The traffic lights became green again, to cross; but neither one accepting the chance to go over and it was safe now, very safe.

"Come on Rudi, let's go". She was verging on anger, resentment even. "What's wrong with you; been on your own too long, too many books, too many dreams you damn fool"!

5

"I thought Sharon was your friend -- how is she"?

"We don't speak now".

"Too bad".

"You jerk"!

The next green light allowed two people to cross the roadway and get into a slow rhythm of pace again. Two ill-crossed youths at another California dusk, with maybe another romantic tragedy in the making. Yet it was more like a Raymond Chandler story, where desperate concerns are pictured upon a leafy scenario of palm-tree boulevards; another disappointing exchange between bodies and dreams, between friends and rivals. Likely these very same scenes were happening in many more small towns, here in California and other states; wherever young people were healthy and free, with the evening climate good and open.

"Afterwards you get a shot, get a fix from the doctor in the morning; you'll be fine".

Rudi left the next piece out, how David was not alright; how he saw his doctor every week and got no remission. "Just can't get rid of this pox", David said to him the week before, when Rudi was looking over his motorcycle as an excuse to visit; still more interested in men and men things.

"I'm not depressed or lonely, you got that! But you say you want me", when she went frontal again; this time with her chest upon his.

"I know when a boy likes me", she explained.

"You know a shot will work okay. You sure"?

She was glad to nod in answer.

"Which doc is that" he said; "what will it cost"?

"Fifty dollars" she said; "just fifty dollars is all".

"Okay" he said, "but"...

"Doctor Farley and really good".

"But, can you loan me? Can you give me the fifty dollars"?

This was the end of the walk, the end of proposals. The girl was very proud as well as available and promising. What she said next did not matter, it was the bigger picture again; another California

6

night and young independence, strength and quarrels. They finally turned completely round for return, to find the two bicycles safe against the railings at the post-office, because it was a small town. The girl said goodnight softly. She said it twice to be sure, before she mounted her ready wheels and he sounded his small bell at her, as he turned off south towards his Beach Road garage.

Still the hurt, confusion, came back to her later; not when alone at night, but next time she met-up with anyone Rudi knew. She was angry enough to spread the word about him and his reluctance, his stubbornness and even spoke to David.

On his part Rudi did not think too much of it and got on his bicycle that night for a quiet ride through the empty town to his rooms, near the beach boardwalk; where the bike went back into the barn made-over to a garage. Rudi checked his big Chevrolet remaining uncovered on the street, then chased up side-steps to low-cost rooms above; where he got ready for a tough day of noise and strain at work, to follow a long level sleep. Back to the cannery for his next shift was to confront truck loads of green sprouts coming into the sheds, every day. He was tired and sore every morning and hard pressed with enough tedium in the week; directing him to another weekend with money in his pockets; to re-engage with his generation at their recreations in a town watering-hole. By Saturday late-evening he was sitting with David in basket chairs, by the bar section, with David throwing peanuts back into his talking gullet and drinking his favourite ale. Rudi's glass was consistently half-full, allowing him to engage talking and listening at the same time.

"She says you turned her down; that's new to her; is how she said it".

"What else she say; why she say that anyway"?!

"Getting back at me, you know, after what I did. But I still got the pox, same as her".

"And more shots, more doctor stuff".

"Why did you do that? We all like her"!

"What you said" --

7

"I mean about the money. She is a lovely lady; no need to make excuses". The conversation moved on, it was all over; a brief accounting without malice and another topic followed without rancor.

Rudi was at work the following week and had dinner at the road-house as before, with the sun hotting up for July and warmer nights. But no more walking-out like the past Friday, because he was going straight over to the tavern after the eats. He never saw the girl at the steak house again, only with the gang at their cafe or down on the beach. By then she seemed okay with Rudi, without grievance or slight, friends as before. In fact he and the girl became better friends by end of summer, because they wanted to make good and catch-up their positions in the group; it was important for them. They rode the bikes together, enjoying a great ocean shore infront of town and sometimes shared food at her place on the cliffs. But no more talk like before. She was ill a long time and her doctor said she may become infertile at end of treatment or have serious blockages from the tissue damage. So said she went into bed at nine-pm each day; because she was scared this time and ate fruit instead of smoking when meeting at the usual places.

And Rudi was meant to be a soldier that year, facing induction into the US forces; when the girl was at the intersection on Front Street that night, arguing for love and peace. He was already in great difficulty with the military obligations and his options. All the western states were gearing up for the Asian war and mobilizing young men between High School and college. By November Rudi had left his job, cleared out his rooms and was driving his Chevy for three days towards Canada and the solution. The girl had taken his bike into her care and wrote to him twice before Christmas, about a new mail-sorting job and news of the friends they had --

"When you coming back; is it possible? David says it's illegal for you to re-enter now. What's it like up there? See any snow"!

In return he described his journey on the road north; the great Redwood trees in Oregon and sleeping in the car overnight. He also said good things about her and the town he missed; so they might not forget, would not forget him. After the New Year he got a clever post-card from them, presenting a strong anti-war sentiment. It was a photo of tombstones headlined as 'the silent majority' – the names of his friends written onto the card on the open stone faces. He turned it over to re-read many times, to see friendship and memories become small and faint: war and relocation, death and separation finally came to the fore for Rudi's generation. He also read how his bike was stolen from her on a trip into town for the bookstore. Rudi did not expect it returned to him, all the way up to Canada; but was not happy the way it was lost so easily and how it involved an unknown person taking it from her.

CHAPTER TWO

He knew this café crowd from before. The mood he encountered in the place was familiar – lazy patrons sitting too long over their coffee with stale conversations and nowhere to go; but the waitress was quick and perky as if to offset the balance. The first thing they each do is look at everybody coming in, check everyone over, as if it was important. Next thing, is see what you ordered, to make a comparison and then feel some failure. Because their attitude was that it was a special undeserved deal, like they could not really afford any service; they somehow had a complex about it. It seemed to him, the mock dramatics he saw had no value and no consequence, when checking over his observations with the glass of water he got infront of him.

So Rudi got his head down over the plate to screen them out, because he really did have something important to do, like eat-up and get going. First he ordered breakfast like he was up all night with something unexpected. It was already three o'clock in the afternoon, but ham-an-eggs was an all-day affair, if you were on the road all week and a long way from the comforts of home...

ROUTE FIVE

Travelling is held to be very American, traveling on wheels across the country; even when you have no good reason and no special place to go. Rudi Borah was late to get his first jalopy, in his twenties; but worth waiting for, because it was like new and very shiny. He heard about the stuff to do on a vehicle; it was popular knowledge, among young men. So he valued the chance to work with automobiles, as a job for a while; it seemed like a good idea. The only station in town, open all night every day, was Richfield gas company where Rudi worked as pump-jockey and garage help. It was a premier lot, with palm trees, a two-tone uniform and the boss all the way from Texas. All alone one night, he took a bid for a wheel-tire from a big man out the valley, who got the flat spare from back of his truck, in June of Nineteen-sixty-nine; when Apollo landed on the moon, the same year Senator Kennedy was shot and Doctor King also killed.

They had a shaggy dog and some paraphernalia gathered from rock concerts and itinerant work, but no kids to really compound their caravan. The big man called his old lady, a fat woman who kept going into the trunk, to bring over some likely tools for straining men at a wheel bench all night. But the man spoke to young Rudi in good humour and overlooked his failing efforts, as the hours went by with no result. The tire machine got a good warm-up as the big man also tried to fit the wrong size and later the right size on the wrong wheel, on a lever unit not a power unit; his wife hovering and waiting for two grown men fix her vehicle so she could go home that night.

The woman went off twice, looking for an eating outlet down the road and got to an adjacent store selling beds in a picture window; still lit-up for late passers-by never heeded by Rudi before. She was forelorn over a pine frame and country linen, behind plate-glass, postered with sales notices and terms. Rudi saw her at the window, as the man kept his back that way to enjoy the slick grease on the wheel nuts and the long pull lever. The men bolstered their patience together over an impossible task, an unlucky woman, a bad wheel and the late night. Nothing else to do but join hands across hard honest steel in the heart of night, swapping strengths and skills to repair a wheel then fit onto his vehicle again; satisfaction with the task completed they head-off before sunrise like he wanted and promised for her. Before they drove away the man suddenly said, "wanna see my new rifle, I got in the back here – a repeating load with wooden stock"! Rudi strolled across the tarmac with him, like he was obliged to --

"I like your yellow Chevie, you got over there, a real vintage vehicle. I can give you this good rifle for it! You're a nice kid. So how about it"? It was all very sudden and Rudi was tired by now.

But he had an 'out' and explained about Canada, the journey he planned to drive next month, how he wanted to visit his parents --.

"Too bad. It's a good deal for an old car".

Rudi liked the man, thinking it the same for him and never guessed he was warming to his vehicle instead. Though this was nothing new for a young man left alone at his station post, keen to satisfy the customers and just as happy to see people by then. But late at night he often encountered lots of enticement, the sort of folly not practised in the rush of daytime duties. A young waitress tried to interest him once, as he washed her volkswagon windows; displaying herself openly and fiddling at her car radio, till he asked for the payment. A smooth looking accountant took a shine to him next, insisting he was very intelligent, good looking and well deserved. Now it was his car -- now someone wanted his vehicle, the first one he ever owned. But in California you spoke your preferences straight away, without any colour of misgivings; no fault in that. Rudi wanted to please the man, after spending all night with him and his wife, though he was shy about telling of his own family commitments.

"Eighteen dollars and gas; that's twenty-four dollars, altogether. Thankyou". Rudi shortened his good-bye but was polite.

"Okay, so long", as the man went off. "You got a great set of wheels there, have yourself a good trip. Might be seeing us again when you get back. Byyeee" and they trundled out to the roadway from the station lot, turning right into the traffic lanes, flashing his lights for everyone to see.

Because it was of mutual benefit Rudi gave a lot of attention to the old saloon car, lots of tuning and service; to get a charging motor, moving, ready for a splendid journey ahead. He was relying upon it to take him north and the vehicle needed a young man at the wheel. Driving through northern California he did not stop, paid no attention to field growers out in the hot sun, viewed from his cab window; in a hurry to get mileage behind him. By the time he got to Oregon the day's sun was too hot to drive, so they stopped at Grants Pass and

13

camped by a river, to let Rudi swim and stretch his long slim frame through clean fresh water. He went to park under a leafy tree and was glad to travel on his own this time; with extra clothing on the rear seat, swim gear, quick-dry briefs and soap. A third day on the road meant a lot of kinks to get out of his system, so Rudi went for backstroke and butterfly returns, for a good hour. Afterwards he got his gear straight back on; no towel needed today, just shorts and blue T-shirt. But after a lot of hard breathing Rudi needed a coffee drink, so he left the auto after re-locking it and walked into town to look for a lunch counter, a low cost unit; stepping into a long place with a lot of chrome, about thirty minutes later --

"You really are my coffee bug", the waitress said to a man next to Rudi.

"What we used to call a germ, now I'm a bug"!

"You really are a sorry soul, so you have to have a donut".

"What kind you got"?

"Every which kind you don't want"!

"Any which way you say, gal". By then she was already looking at Rudi, "hi there. What's your choice? Coffee"?

"And a milkshake".

"A shake and coffee -- yeah"?

"Yes, that's it".

"Not with a donut, I hope, pal".

"Sorry which way he ain't, for sure, you copy big guy"?

Then they brought Rudi into the joke, while the owner sat apart reading a newspaper and watching. They were now four of them, but still only two talking. Rudi was part of the group, but not trying any table-talk like that, though he enjoyed hearing it. The girl was a model working teenager and would not see the man outside the café, maybe not even recognize him if he occupied another seat. She was very trim in yellow rayon, with waistband and soap-an-water makeover, like other girls at the tables. Altogether, they were a smart group; a lot like the pump boys at Rudi's station in another town, another state. They kept right on talking as he began to drink and she

14

waited-on a long shiny counter with four more customers and the owner-man at counter's end. It was a lot of action for a small café, in a small town. But Rudi was loathe to leave the place when the man next to him shook his hand and the gal quickly waved, because he wanted to see what would happen --

He got back to the river in good time to find his vehicle still safe upon return, waiting in the shade and facing northward for him. When Rudi first took ownership of the used sedan he was in San Cutraz in work, flush with five hundred dollars and a new state's vehicle license. By the time he gave it a test ride he forgot about other items on the sales lot and let the dealer talk him into it; who said one previous owner, low mileage and warranty. It was a week before he took it over forty-mph and he kept it off the freeway for one more week. Of course he was repaid with mobility and dates, in a roomy chromed two-tone cruiser, looking very impressive when sat at the kerbside. Wendy had the main benefit at that time, when she got Rudi to take her drinking or cruising their town beyond the curfew, while she exhausted her cigarettes or exhausted the excitement by keeling over on the rear seat. He tried to kiss her once, when she was enjoying a cigarette in her fingers around his head and burned his ear. No small irony, which Rudi acted upon, when he deferred her joy-riding treats and also took ownership of a bicycle that year.

Rudi journeyed up to Canada to see his mother who was unwell and his step-father needing help that summer. He had agreed and promised her; gave notice at the gas-filling station and made ready for a four-day drive north in the month of July; with some savings, a serviced automobile and clean gear. He saw Wendy the last Saturday before going and chanced her a ride in the front seats, as she rapped on about her strict father and absent mother; then about school, where she was fixated upon the new socials teacher from San Diego. Rudi was in an awkward position when he saw how mixed-up she was after her parents divorce and how the teacher was a gay from Mexico. He was glad to be going north awhile and gave it a corollary value of separation involving parents again, his parents. She did not unravel that night and he dropped her at home, still leaning his way, as she registered a pathway to the door and did all the waving as he drove off.

Reaching Oregon, he went through the famed giant sequoia redwoods; big red trees covering the hills with a very high canopy from firm ground below, clear of brush and debris; very unlike second-growth at a logging site. The trees were well placed and spaced like Kings and Queens of the forest: big, silent and russet red. A lot of other timber species were missing, birds were very high and the sparse cover below did not encourage life on the forest floor – it was a walled enclosure like a cathedral space, with less noise, more cover, less light.

The road went through this terrain for hours till he drove on into darkness. So by eleven-pm he pulled over to sleep in a subordinate parking lot at a truck stop. He slowed up quietly and dimmed the headlights, as he stopped beneath furthest lights on the lot and got ready to crash-out on the back seat. First, he got out the vehicle to walk a few steps into more darkness; to relieve himself before sleeping and inhaled thick pine fragrances mixed with newly oxygenated air. The lords of the forest were not red now, but dark black columns going up into another dark mass overhead. The air was motionless, but an owl hooted its night signal to say it could see him but not the reverse; a sign for Rudi to retreat and sleep in a most favoured state, suitably tired, suitably accomodated.

Next morning the road was one day closer to Canada, the border crossing and Bellingham to Blaine; Bellingham harbour on Puget Sound and Blaine a hitch stop just before the crossing; with a sample of diversions, blue movies, long-hour drinking and poker tables. The sheriff's cruiser waited at the hitching rail at front of the postal service; the attending deputy outfitted in a grey suit with side-arm, bare arms and heavy middle, stomping between his hard-top and the refreshment licenses. Rudi stepped upon the board sidewalk and entered a café-bar to sit awhile over a table spread of warm food; the safest way to enter a strange area where he was perceived as unknown and untested. But he was tested, so too was his vehicle and they were known at his mother's house in Canada; known in another town other side of the border – past the big Peace Arch structure five miles out of Blaine -- hosting lots of border-pigs, flags, rows of traffic cones and end of journey --

Highway Five went to Canada from California, Oregon, then Washington State. It was a straight road north which continued all the way up to Alaska, called the Al-Can highway. He continually thought of this as he sat in his own auto and stared ahead over the steering; stared at the white marks along the asphalt, like it was a flight path. His trusty machine sped along the road as the engine torque developed through gears and transmission; the carriage was pulled along by friction and pushed ahead by combustion. By the time Rudi worked this out he started looking for off-ramp refreshment; looking out for the high sign-poles which read, Gas/Food/Bed.

He also thought about the cars infront and behind; if they might be on an important journey or a good ride -- impossible to know, even when he followed the same vehicle many hours or saw the full-face of another driver. No one had contact with anyone else, after a quick glance at each other. A fat lady was with him all the way from Redding to Yreka. She looked over once, messed with her hair every half-hour and sang to the car radio, because her lips moved but no one with her. A produce truck was with him in Oregon and its side-paint said 'Arizona oranges' and 'tomatoes from Mexico'. It went about seventy-mph and swung about the lanes in an excellent pattern for hills and gradients, as effective speed and safety. Two highway patrols flowed easily by him and buses of various orange/yellows traversed his route all through the day. He was content with the mechanics of driving and busy with the diverting images competing for his attention. The driving was really a minimal activity, which required a lot of empty attention to be filled with worries and speculation, fantasy and fear. At start of journey the movement was smooth and comfortable, but as the hours passed this was not important, other concerns came to the fore.

He held a steady speed of sixty-five to seventy-mph and moved between the middle and outside lanes, going another four hours on the driving seat. He learned to shift his rear round the bench seat every thirty minutes or so, as he re-adjusted the windows, sun-visor, pedals and panel levers. He allowed the front-right floor to hold rubbish and waste after he ate an orange, nuts and chocolate; the rear seat taking folded blankets, books and clothes, a shelf of pack-sack items. This shelf included more chocolate, more fruit and packets of salted nibbles; solitary eats for lonesome pleasures. But the movement made it all worth-while: the sweet liberty of leaving problems behind, leaving people and routines; leaving behind stale rooms, daily work, low pay and maybe a bit of boredom or loneliness. Until Rudi stopped the motor and landed his cruiser at a terminus; when it would be new people and new problems. But till then he was moving, moving between them, moving fast or slow it was not unpleasant and brought its own special colours of freedom; freedom from this and that, or the freedom to do something different. The other concern was to cover ground, a lot of ground; like native Indians did last century on foot or on horseback. When it was primitive instinct to make a mark, make an impression upon the land, as the wolf marks out a territory. To travel a land freely was like owning it --

"Yes sir – what'd'yuh need", came from the pump stand?

"Just gas, gas please. Fill her up". Rudi eased to a halt at a quiet station to punctuate the distance he planned.

"And can I check your oil"?

"Don't bother; well alright, go ahead. But I wash my own windows. Thanks".

The attendant recognized the Mercury and before he could lift his head to ask, Rudi helped him out -- "it's a Fifty-five, a Nineteen-fifty-five model".

"Great year for Mercury Monterey; a classic, V8 engine"!

"Over three hundred horse power, I think".

"A real ladies car; a pick-up bus. Right"?

"No, just a gas guzzler. This land cruiser is a self-abuser for me and a wall-flower with the girls".

"Maybe it's a man's car these days, what with the vintage appeal an-all; a great man's motor – yeah"!

"Who knows; I only own and drive it; am'not a collector. But we take no malice".

The man checked the ties while Rudi wiped the windows and took stock of mixed surroundings he saw; with his ticket to ride – freedom of the road – a basic constitutional liberty. That's what Henry Ford was remaking – the rights of liberty for individuals -- as good business.

"Where you from, not round here, that's for sure"?

"The Mid-West, back east! Sorry, I just came up from California, that's south".

"You going to Canada"?

"How'd'you know that"?

"That's how far a full tank will take you. Right up to Bellingham and more".

"Yeah; it's that close here"!

"Up that on-ramp north. Point your figure on the hood this side of Mount Baker and keep the Straits on your left side".

"I might come-by on the return trip. See you then"!

"There's no need son, it's okay".

"Bye" -- as Rudi motored out gently as possible, letting the man linger on the sight of new youth in an old wagon; no need to spook him twice like that. Rudi knew it was in cherry condition and the man much younger when it was last seen; like it was a ghost out for an evening haunt and in the hands of an impostor. But he raised the speed after a traffic stop and did not look back.

By nine-pm he was squared away on the Olympic Coast, upon a cliff level at the harbour; where he could follow the sun to bed across the sea, when last red colours were squashed across the level waters. His car was still warm from the day's sun and the engine heat. Rudi sat on soft ground against the driver's door, to face a dying western sky, with no food or drink left to think of. This was not like driving, when consciousness filled with competing concerns; now there was no competition with the goodnight sun and display of red shades. Everything was up-graded in full colour, till advancing shadows finally won over the evening scene. Rudi was happily insignificant before a great light show and it was his own show, seen only from this rock platform tonight; a singular audience at a gala performance of astra-opera. He had his back against flat panel metal, legs in front on clean dark earth and listened for a murmuring heart beneath his folded arms, till an appointed hour on his wrist-watch. No other way to end all of this.

Rudi owned an automobile long before he owned a house, before he married or became a father. He got a driver's license soon after High School and worked to support his vehicle without complaint. He was a good owner/driver, which required him hold a job to take care of it and saw the dangers first time out, did not have an accident for four years. Though he never had savings anymore, he never lost his ignition keys and the highway patrols usually let him alone.

CHAPTER THREE

A little girl was playing in the park because it was August, when days were hot and sunny. She had a plastic bucket and spade; the bucket a fire-engine red and the spade was blue-an-yellow. The child had a game figured out, in her own mind; about emptying the pond onto the sidewalk with her bucket and poking her spade at gold fish in the depths, trying to reach them. The fish were big creatures, a little fat and slow, with all those bread crumbs and tit-bits thrown to them by on-lookers. But they stayed in the deepest parts of the water, to be safe and waited till the girl would leave. Leaves in the trees above were in full summer growth, fluttering with the breeze, making some comfortable shade for her. By late afternoon it was still very warm and the child wore no clothes, naked like the day she was born, standing in the shallows; when a policeman arrived. The officer was wearing a dark-blue uniform with cap and looked at her in surprise. He didn't know what to do, except to keep saying: "where's your mother? Is anyone taking care of this child", glancing round at people nearby? The girl stood quiet and still, very proud of her bucket-an-spade she held onto; looking at him straight and calm; because she knew exactly what to do on such a lovely day.

A BOY'S OWN

Boys have a long way to go and a lot to do, to make people happy. A boy must travel far, or at least dream like this and not be afraid to leave home; so he has to start young, soon as possible. Older men and women can help, because they are free, because they can be patient and gentle.

Rudi was a good boy and because he was so young, just gone ten, he was also obedient. Not to his father, because he kept well out the way with a job and his own thoughts. He was obedient to his mother, who sent him to his grandmother and obedient to his maternal grandmother when she sent him to her husband, his retired grandfather; a government officer most of his life and head of a successful household as old-style patriarch. His grandmother set him down on a stool in front of an evening fire opposite his grandfather. But first he ate dinner with them and enjoyed a different recipe and no parents. Then his grandfather went out the kitchen over to a sparking fire and got out a briar pipe to wait for the boy. He was keen to tell about Napoleon and other old soldiers. Rudi was attentive because he enjoyed these stories. The old man was a good story-teller and the grandmother came by to see how the boy was faring. All the stories were of battles in war, battles on sea or land, in the nineteenth century. Grandpa liked props and moved the salt and pepper shakers round a table top, or drew troop lines across the hearth tiles; puffing his pipe smoke and took the boy backwards to a fabled land of horses and flags, men without comforts, colour and danger.

"Now Rudi did I tell you about Nelson? Lord Nelson of the King's navy"! The boy was embarrassed to answer, but knew he would enjoy the same story again. It was going to be a little different this time anyway; the old man knew how to make a good story new again.

"Well, Nelson was only a little man, very short you know. But he showed 'em, even when he had no arm and one eye, he still showed 'em and won the day; even the last day when he lay dying, he won the battle. Yeah, no eye and no arm became useful you know. How he put the spyglass to his blind eye and disobeyed superior orders to disengage the enemy; then went on to win the battle, defeat the French Navy at the Battle of the Nile"!

Rudi showed silent enthusiasm on his stool, but was tired by end of day and had to really sit-up and look well. His grandfather kept on a full hour or more, while his grandmother began washing dishes and singing to herself in the kitchen. The boy never asked questions, but did try some short answers through the period and knew it was important to the elder man; because his wife in the kitchen was nervous about disturbing them at the hearthside. Rudi's mother spoke strongly about these sessions with her father, how she hated it. How he could be a terrible man with his job, habits and story lessons of history; how his mother now disliked any history or any tale from her father the family head.

The other stories were from his own work career in City Hall as head of welfare. How he had to deal with town politicians on his committee, the sad clients he saw, the violent ones. He had lots of tales to tell, which he needed to make humorous or triumphant for a small boy. Rudi remembered it was like History; but he was concerned to hear of career difficulties, troubles at work, from a near relative. The stories were shortened and dramatized, for a grandson, not like they really happened; but the tone was there, anxiety and cruelty, disappointment and anger – but no failure. The man in front of Rudi was not triumphant, not a model hero; but he saw it all through and was before Rudi laughing and smoking, with a good woman in the kitchen. Though the grandfather could not be sure, it was also important to the boy, same as the history accounts and his grandmother echoed the career issues he made. Even his mother knew his own stories to be true and protested briefly.

"Is it time Rudi went home"?

"Yes Ernie".

"What time you in bed, Rudi"?

"Eight o'clock and nine o'clock on weekends".

"What about Sunday"?

"Eight o'clock – because school is next day".

"Had enough to eat, have yuh? What about some cake before you go"?

"No, Ernie, too late now"!

"You want to hear about Julius Caesar, again"?

Rudi sat between them, to see what was decided and it was one more story, a short one; then off home to the next street but one.

"Our girl will wonder where the lad is", came from the kitchen.

"You heard of Rome and the Roman Empire"? He asked,

relighting the tobacco in his pipe. "Well Caesar was the Emperor; he was a great soldier but ambitious, hard on his men".

"Yes, I remember", Rudi added.

"Good lad; alright. You also remember what he did after he landed his army in Britain"?

"He burnt all the ships".

"That's right – so no way back".

"So the soldiers would have to fight harder".

"Right again; well done! Yuh see, those wild and ugly ancient Brits really scared the hell out of the Romans, the regular legionaries; yes they did"! There was a lot more free commentary like this, till it was time for him to go --

By eight o'clock Rudi went out the door to go home and he was tired; but important for him to hear all this once, twice, three times. He knew it was going to be important one day. His grandpa thought it was and Rudi agreed that when he grew up he'd need to know this sort of stuff. His mother was extra considerate by the time he arrived home and he went to bed without any fuss, head full of lessons, full of warnings and the smoke and smell of a man with his first grandson.

All this carried on for years, but the boy enjoyed it and accepted the time as essential. It was the oral tradition of one man and his time to benefit another branch of his spreading family. About once a week he would be at the fire, on a stool and given special treatment to follow from the two women who leant him to the sessions. His house was only twenty minutes from his grandmother, so in winter he still went for the dinner and the talk. He tried to enjoy the food, a strange contrast to his mother's dishes and pretended to be tired then awake at the same time. He was a little confused sometimes and pretended to be hungry then interested in narrative history again.

The props his grandfather used also told stories: table-ware items were wedding gifts, the stool came from an old dairy farm and their house was colonial style. For a long time Rudi kept doing what his mother asked and what his grandmother wanted. His grandfather

24

went on to produce four more grandsons and a granddaughter; but they never got any lessons at the fire, only the first grandchild because the next children lived far away and the old man passed his best. But he loved his grandson because he listened, never to know if he understood or would benefit later. He loved a boy who was not unlike him and later the boy loved his own child. Rudi had his child at an older age; a late child for him and he loved his girl same as the old man would. But it was not a boy, so no stories, no pipe-smoking or history.

At school, History was quite different; no battles and no Caesar. It was governments and dates, reading and a lot of writing. His teacher, Mr. Morrison, was veteran of World War Two; rumours were he had serious injuries and was a hero. He said, "what makes men go to war" and "what makes a nation declare peace"? Rudi always forgot, untill he heard it again, after a suitable rebuke from the teacher. He remembered the answers one at a time and was disappointed after being a good student with his grandfather.

"Men go to war, because, because they want to. And..."

"And armies declare peace when the money runs out", Thomas called out from back of the class. He always knew these answers. By then Rudi had answers for the next questions – "Why does a nation-state want war"?

"People are made to think it will be short and decisive"!

"What belies the difference between the two" Mr. Morrison continued?

"Ministers are empowered to spend taxes and men must be tricked into leaving home", Rudi called out without signal.

"Good lad! We have a humanitarian at our side and an historian at the back. But both are boys"!

No matter, because History was a poor second at school for Rudi; already a charter member of the geography club on Fridays. Mr. Stonebridge was resident explorer-teacher and organizer of adventure trails. Saturday coming they were meeting at the school field to head out for the day; trail-finding and mapping. Rudi's friend was the same, always there for the day out; the play away from home and they walked over together at eight-am that morning, checking their lists and guessing on tasks for the day.

"No girls want to come", repeated Thomas every week.

"Two or three were talking about it at school".

"They don't count; you heard about 'tom-boys' haven't you"?

"Girls are okay; your sister is a girl, so are two of my cousins. They show in pants when I visit and are game to join in".

"You don't get it Rudi; you got tom-boy cousins"!

"Hey, we're going to the beach today" --

"What for"?

"Making a chart of the tide changes" --

Mr. Stonebridge was shouting all the way from school to the rocks, because he said they were not safe. Then they went in groups of eight, at different ends of the beach. Rudi was opposite Thomas awhile, at foot of the east bank as leader and gave out items to carry. He had to manage a rolled tape to measure the surface, starting at high tide mark up on the shingle; where sand grass had dried and lying above thick wet healthy waterweed. Different kinds of shingle marked a tide-line too. It seemed to be starting to make sense today. By noon Rudi was ready for any kind of sandwich in his tin; his mother had included peanut-butter and chocolate cookies – standard fare for a game boy. He also had a flask of milk and raisins and afterwards went over to Thomas about his lunch and their measurements.

"I told you Rudi – no girls here today".

"Maybe they have something better to do".

"Shopping I suppose! What d'you think"?

"I don't think; but why do you care"?

"No; you're the one who cares – stupid"!

They were also keen to battle with sand and water, to get their task done. And next a free-for-all to find crabs, in the tide pools, before setting off home. It was windy and bright by afternoon and their teacher saw they all looked a bit frazzled from exposure at water's edge, out of season and untested. But the boys were successful and safe today. Next year was High School and new choices; some lads would likely choose more geo-sciences, he was thinking.

"I'm home; anybody home"! Rudi got straight to the kitchen without taking his coat off because he needed to find someone. There were papers left open and a jacket on the chair, cups left out; so Rudi trailed round to back of the house to see his father in the garden. He found it in his father's face when he got there, recognition of boy out in the world, to make extra points towards their relationship. Then Rudi suddenly switched his attention, "where's my mother"?

"You hungry Rudi? Get a sandwich from the fridge; I don't want it". He continued with the string and cutters among the rows of beans; happy because he knew what he was doing. Rudi did not, because his mother was missing and his father busy.

"Your mother's not here, but wants to talk with you". He stood up to turn around and seemed to repeat this with the glance he gave Rudi, who could not answer. The Saturday beach exercise was obviously not important now and adults were fickle with children.

When his mother never returned by late evening, his father said he had to work and she went to the hospital; so they decided Rudi must stay round the corner, stay at his grandparents place. In fact, he had to go tonight after his mother did not come back from the doctor that day; instead, she went straight to a maternity unit. It puzzled him, when asked to lodge at his grandparent's house, as if he didn't want to go. They said a weekend, or a bit longer. Of course it was longer – a week. This time, it led to a different kind of conversation with them, a new interest in the boy --

"What do you want Rudi"?

"Not sure".

"You want a brother to play with"!

"I think so".

"He plays alright with his cousins, Ernie"!

He went to school from a different direction and enjoyed finding a new way to the gates, through a graveyard adjacent to the football

27

field; a nice walk through lines of elm trees and daisy lawns between the headstones. He came back that way too, though it began to darken after school; wind would sound amongst the trees, transforming the place and making it a little scary. Each evening he had the same kind of dinner; potatoes and bread with gravy, then custard. His grandfather always took tea and biscuits in front of the hearth fire, where they were ready to talk. Every day was a comfortable routine, which ended in an old bedroom full of dark furniture, dark corners, old magazines to look at. He always forgot about a baby by the evening; difficult for a boy to think of having a brother or sister to share his room, his belongings. So he let the adults do all the thinking and all the guessing. By the time he was to go home again and leave his grandparents he wanted to stay, because there was a lot of fuss going on and he was nervous about the upheaval and the excitement in adults.

The first day home Rudi went walking a lot, down to the river where he thought it good to be very serious, looking at the moving water and bits of background. He did it often this year, after Mr. Stonebridge took his club along the river, to show how wonderful it really was. He wanted to see what this meant, how a flow of muddy water was special, when not even fish were using it these days. He sat down on a grassy bank adjacent to the bridge, not to attract attention, most of the morning. It was Sunday, a good day for a boy to get lost safely; getting lost in a useful way, an important way. The water was a solid colour of dark brown and one or two tree branches followed the surface in front of him, then under the bridge span. But looking at it long enough was still not 'Huck Finn' on the Mississippi River. Huck was lost and glad of it, Rudi was only lost. By this stage he got up and walked along the bank; the movement always made things brighter. He decided to return home again. He often left home like this for a few hours and felt to be far away as he sat or strolled the river path. In his heart he had left home, had run away; but after a while knew he was not ready and they were not ready. One day he must go, he already knew that, though it troubled him why and where.

His mother saw the look on his face as he came into the house; she usually tried to speak to him and it did not help. "Cheer up Rudi. Hungry; tired! You can talk to me".

"What"!

"Some big news; you have a new sister. Come on take a look at her"!

"Where"?

He was led into a bedroom to see a bundle of white garments around a small object in a cradle. He took a look at a baby with sore cheeks, frizzy hair and eyes closed. He knew it was too much for him, so after a short time he went into his own room to look for a bat and ball, see if they were still there. Nothing changed in his room he was glad to see; nothing changed yet and realized he had another reason why not to leave home. The next week he often peered into the crib, to see the baby cry when awake or eyes closed when silent. Then school caught up with him again; how he wanted to make friends with the mathematics teacher, so maths would be more friendly with him. Mr. Rowenstein was easy to find at end of day, in Rm-13, with posters of maths prodigies upon the walls alongside some famous number puzzles. He wore eye-glasses, of course and a checked shirt.

"Keen all of a sudden Rudi, what's wrong? Tell me"?

"Nothing".

"But never saw you last term. I took you for an out-doors man; yes I did".

"No change really. Just need to get better scores".

"Well, join the crowd, please do. Every Thursday at four-pm; my Maths Club. You already have a pal here, I can see you do", as another boy went up close to them both.

"Hi Rudi, glad to see you here. It's a good club; really helps".

"How'd'you know"?

"I been here the whole semester. My grades are up and parents off my case"!

"It would help with other courses; don't forget that boys", as Mr.

Rowenstein moved away, back to his own tidy desk. Tom stepped the other way and let his books close, "Rowenstein is alright; he likes you".

"How so"?

"Because I talk so much, he gets nervous. Hey, how the gals treating you, your cousins I mean"?

"Alright".

"You have to say that, becos you're such a 'home-boy', straight from the country cabin". Tom was familiar with the club and his standing, enough so he could show off. "I can help you with stuff, this time anyway".

But Thomas could not help after Rudi got bronchitis again that season and was confined to his room a week and inside the house another week. No school and no clubs, no extras that term. He was used to all this and got out the extra pajamas and house-robe as inevitable sequence of events. He had long coughing through the nights, yet by mid-day was ready to get up and go downstairs; each day like this as if there had been a mistake and the doctor wrong about him. How well he felt when sitting inside the window to see how life was outside -- the mail-man at their gate with his heavy bag, the sound of vehicles next street over -- the sense of men working in the background and women in full voice at town. Not so bad to be ill or inside the house but he was missing out; not too young to know that or feel it. A boy must not be kept back or kept from things, like his grandfather had instructed. Rudi learned something about himself that month, that he had many miles to go, long travels ahead; even though he would not begin till after school, he already worried about standing still, about not moving. Rudi had a fear of lassitude and weakness, long before he knew about journeys and distance. Seems some things come backwards to a boy, whether it's fair or not.

He had a model sailboat in his room which got more attention at such times; lemon drinks on a tray and a new book from his grandfather; but no visitors in his room because of the coughing. There were no half-measures and nothing spared as he was the first grandson, the first son; to carry forward the masthead of family themes and quests. Very often, Rudi could feel the stress of adult conversations: the firm dictates, some tense silences and awkward responses – as a repeating pattern to follow. Long past concerns were passed onto the small and innocent, the same way young birds learned to migrate or fox-cubs learned to hunt. The sense of it was stronger than when it was understood years later. It was complicated to be a boy after the war, because there were too many baby-boomers and too many boys. These issues were underlined as this lad was declared unwell and not allowed outside.

CHAPTER FOUR

The next bout was on Friday evening and it would be ten rounds against a slugger from San Jose. He was at his best weight and a good height against the visitor; twenty-five years old with six contests under his belt. But when the fight started he began back-peddling and counter punching. His trainer was yelling to go forward, seeing him shy and cautious, looking to perfect his defense. On the stool between rounds, he took another pounding from his own seconds, about attacking his opponent.

For the first five rounds the lad from Sacramento defended superbly, but was losing on points. He was composed and fresh like the beginning, dancing around the ring – till a blow on the nose closed both eyes and started a trickle of blood across his upper lip. He had been hurt and embarrassed infront of the home crowd, getting tagged like an amateur. Now he was angry, so went after the opponent, trying to get even. He forgot about fancy footwork for fans at the front, forgot about his corner, the purse money or what day-ofth-week it was. Now he was upset, a new kind of energy came after weeks of training – the early morning road work, a bit of rough sparing, some furious skipping and going at the punch-bag. His trainer now backed-off and kept quiet, folded his bare arms infront and puffed at a cigar. Next time, on the stool, he was soothing and reassuring with his charge: "take it easy, kid, we're scoring good. Just put him away when you're ready".

SURVEY TIME

Men without women are a crazy lot, like when it's a war or in a prison. It begins for good purpose, for a job, big wages; a means to an end. But this is soon forgotten and the women are forgotten too, not needed much. When these two do get together again there's trouble; because men have to climb down to learn something old and forgotten and women grieve over the lost time.

It was four-pm when Rudi got to camp, to be ready for the next morning. By the evening six young men were gathered and talking into the night, about last season mostly and events in town. Next day they were to travel to Indian land on the river, where survey sections would be assigned to pairs of the crew. The rest of the evening he tried to get ready for a six month job with no frills, no comforts and high pay. He took out a shirt and socks, put them on the chair for morning and had a leisurely shave in the basin before sleeping.

Rudi had driven an old station-wagon from town up to the hills and thought about what he left behind, what may come next. The landscapes were nothing special till about four thousand feet; when he could see sheer rock faces, a snow glacier and long green lakes; passing logging crews off the roadside where men were year-round at forestry. He called at a road-stop cafe to get some flavour of the area and sat thirty minutes in a quiet place, a traditional back-water rendezvous; so men could shout across to each other about different jobs and how the environment went against them at season changes. There was a set of antler horns upon the wall and dark stained timbers, cafe stuff and pie. The vehicles parked on the lot were mostly four-wheeled drive with flat beds, because these men had to work for a living, not up for skiing; rough work mostly and dangerous, which effected the way they talked -- loud and firm.

Back on the road to the survey camp Rudi was beginning to feel comfortable about working with new help, college boys from the city, working and bunking till fall. There was to be one boss from the state department and four trailers on the site for sleeping quarters and equipment. First meal on the job was wieners/beans, bread, tinned fruit and milk -- basic eats for crew boys. Later, lots of men-talk went till lights-out; then coffee and eggs in the morning. That first week Rudi got an Irish youth and they talked a lot without reserve, shared the coffee and sprayed each other with the same insect repellent. Patrick was a four-year agronomy student and dairy

34

farmer's son who knew cows and fields but not forests. He was four years younger than Rudi, fatter and happier.

The second week was with another farmer's son, Gavin, who looked like German descent. He was real serious about the work and his tidy world which went no further than state lines; outside this haven was confusing and irrelevant far as he was concerned. They dug holes and marked aerial photos for soil mapping; which was a priority this year as of Federal funds. The work was tedious and dirty, but enjoyable for young men who still wanted to try themselves in a wild environment, on a hot mountain and end up with a good grub-stake in September.

They all disliked the mosquitoes and united in efforts against them, they went together on food and drink and chores, but nothing else. Nothing else seemed to matter for them, enough to stop them fighting, arguing; many serious dislikes to cause every offense and young blood, new egos, needed lots of action results. They weren't good at coping with the heat like they thought and no good without girls to take notice. Mosquitoes were not stopped and kept at crews in the greener shades, all season long, feeding on this hot young blood and getting fat. But maps were developed and records compiled; the boss grinned each day at the full compliment of help with no one falling away.

"Come on Rudi, yuh sore head. We all got hard ground to cover. Keep your philosophy to yourself -- no one knows the answers anyway. Sure as hell you don't"!

"Who I got today"?

"Edward, you got Ed. Get down the river this morning and finish-up; then up Fraser Ridge to get some trenches dug, for the soil profiles. I'll be by to look-see later".

"Get the tools Ted, will yuh; I mean things for digging". Rudi was starting off right. "The map stuff is with me" --

"What about gas and water"?

"Good thinking, Teddy bear"!

First chance to go home, when crews left for the weekend, Rudi did not go with them. He stayed on site, operated alone and spent his time slowly attending chores to help him listen, to help think. No travelling home next weekend either, because he didn't want to travel back umpteen times in the summer. He wanted to be up there in his forest sanctuary, not for the pay, not the job; he wanted hard time to work something out. Each day he hit the brush with a lot of gusto; swinging his machete like it was a tennis racket and sweeping cobwebs with the other hand; directly away from the truck for hours, when they went to dig at the river. They trodded the undergrowth like it was wading water; through deep layers of rubbish piled up from years of decaying forest. It was hot and dusty with legions of insects at the skin -- just what young men like for a while after too many years inside school, too many years at home. Rudi wore two shirt layers and long sleeves to prevent bites, which were unfailing and unpleasant under the forest canopy out of direct sunlight. Rudi and Edward squatted against tree trunks with sandwiches at noon; to see mosquitoes get to knees and elbows, where they attacked through patches of taught khaki. But these mites were counted and hit for idle amusement, when they bit and sucked at the resting hosts.

"What you doing next year, Rudi"?

"Next year! You mean this year, after the job finishes"?

"Yeah".

"Get a new truck, visit Hawaii, go to Europe. I dunno".

"This is my last year at college, in September".

"I was glad to leave High school; but that's years ago. I like the forest; I like good pay and outdoors work, yeph, I really do".

"I'm going into food labs; my brother is senior technician. He got married with a kid now".

"That's great".

"When you gonna get married, Rudi"?

"I dunno, after I get the truck; after a trip to Mexico, Europe is too far. I need an education yer know".

"Well, it's my last summer up here with these bugs".

"Lots of bugs in town for yuh; some with four legs if you want!

Think of the bigger picture; think of ten, twenty years ahead".

"I think you really like this place; or is it the work, a place to think and be alone. Which is it"?

But they were friends and glad of it; happy with a raw environment which demanded obvious strengths and sure relations with working mates; a clear picture and clear results for young men in a new country. Food mattered but money didn't, friendship mattered but advancement didn't, comfort mattered but not too much. The air was fresh, talk was free and the season not too long. Then Rudi sought a southern horizon before winter closed in. He planned a round trip away from the state, because he had been successful, flushed with good standing and funds. California was appealing and far enough away to be different.

"Come on Ted, that's enough, let's go"!

"I might change my course; it's been the best summer so far. What d'you say to that"?

"Same as end of last season"!

"Maybe forestry would be better; lot'a big outfits in the state now. Those stores and farms too small -- you think"?

"Maybe food not so important, eh! Come on, drive will yuh. Go. Go"!

San Francisco was different; far enough away to be nothing like what he heard. Rudi had three weeks of the Fall in North Beach and enough dollars to troll the Wharf and Broadway, looking for excitement and diversion. But the residents were looking for the same thing and seemed to think Rudi was the answer; he such an innocent, raw working boy out from the woods. So that by the end Rudi was glad to leave and start work with another crew in another territory; but not till end of the month. That evening he was still out on the streets --

"Hey, where you from" she said? "Not round here that's for sure"!

"Canada".

"That's north of California, way up by Oregon right? Wow"!

"No -- further up".

"What'you'do up there on a winter night? You have to really get together, yeah"?

Rudi was at Fisherman's Wharf on an evening tour and hesitated at a street stall attended by a hippie chick. She was pretty but smoked furiously.

"You from here"?

"No, Walnut Creek; a real snotty area and so unreal, I had to leave. I met my ole-man at Junior college and we came to the city last summer. My mom's a doctor and she wanted to bust him"!

"Why here"?

"This is where it's at. My man really digs it. So we got into a house on Pacific Beach, but we have to share".

"What's he do, the boyfriend I mean"?

"He's into music, heavy metal. And he plays wind stuff to get into a band maybe". By now the girl was through a third cigarette on her stool, amid a litter of butts and ash. Rudi leaned against the wood uprights opposite her.

"I mean about work"?

"Oh, okay -- he's in a leather store, making belts and sandals. Really cool gear for the local heads and anyone turned-on by what's happening".

"He make any chastity belts? -- Ooophs, sorry"!

"No, sex is groovy. So is grass. We do both together, it's really far out. A great trip".

"I don't smoke".

"You look like you'd be good on grass; I can tell. You can smoke with us, it's organic".

Rudi started to cut it short because she was on work-time, selling at a booth till very late. But Rudi was on open-time, in a welcome warm evening, so he stood up straight again to walk off.

"I have to go. What's your name, by the way"? A great smile burst from Rudi as he turned away to nowhere in particular and kept at an even pace away from the water, from the booths and the smoking girl, for a new direction. But he wanted to remember her.

Before beginning work again he got down to the bar for a more common diversion -- beers and strippers. It was a big beer parlour off the North Side highway, next to a rail terminal, so no local residents to stifle ongoings at the place. Rudi and Gavin met in the parking lot, then went shyly to a side-door entrance. Gavin managed to find a table and make an order, above the sudden noise-din, which hit them hard even in the furthest reaches of the place. Before they downed first drinks a girl was announced and appeared on the raised stage area. She came on in a sequined two-piece, red with white fringe and the 'Bee Gees' thumping their material for a bar dance. Rudi was back of the bar and washed down two glasses of lager before he dared look hard across the stage, at Tina; a half-breed Indian gal taking her clothes off the third time tonight, first time for Rudi and made a convincing show across a whole arena of flim-flam. By the second tune Rudi took Gavin closer and they saw a tall woman looking her best for a group of riff-raff infront. She twisted and turned every-which-way and slid over the boards to the youngest guy who waved a dollar bill for her. It was easy to step into this bar, drink and watch; it was also stupid and difficult to go to bed alone after a head full of ready women.

Tina proffered a smile at the two men and talked back to the boys at the front rail.

"Come over here to get this; we don't bite".

"We-ll, tha-annkk-youu"…

"We only want your body; no problems with that. Who knows you're a nice person, or whatever" --

"This is too small, boys", tossing her head back. "I need a ten or twenty"!

But Rudi got an eye-full of ripe flesh, young face and at the end a photo-card with number to call, spun out to him by Tina as an encore. He stood it next to a time-piece in his room where it stayed for weeks. There was also Anita a red-head and Ruby an Asian lady. But Gavin insisted they were all the same; how Rudi was looking for the same woman every time and that it was stupid and obvious. Rudi argued they really fancied him, but were constrained by conventions, even though he passed notes back-stage --

"Hi Tina,

want some coffee!?

Let's meet at the c-shop,

see you in 10 minutes.

...Rudi (in checked coat).

PS -- great dancing".

He always went the extra distance, at work in the bush or with writing letters back home:

"Hi Mom,

okay job I got. Extra big check this week,

but hot and dusty and tired!

Can I bring home some washing?

-- bring my friend Gavin?

-- borrow father's auto?

Missing you...

Rudolph.

PS -- I mean next month not this week".

Of course Mom and Tina could not compete with Marian, who was not family and not out-of-reach. She came to Rudi via Gavin and someone else Rudi worked with; a young woman who kept appearing on the scene, who was emerging. They got on well because he only saw her weekends and one evening. He maintained his own space and rarely talked of love or the future; keeping to the wider ground of mutual friends, respectful distance and certain pleasures. Likely his father would be curious and his mother satisfied to see a younger woman with straight job and no ragged edges. To keep a good balance Rudi declared that it just happened and meant no changes. He enjoyed a regular woman, but wanted some control, which caught the admiration of his gang for a while. Rudi liked to be a rebel and the outsider; which made an awkward place in-between for Marian and she knew it.

By Christmas Marian went to Rudi's place and made him suppers on Saturday night and sometimes breakfast. He got so bold as to call her his 'ole-lady' and got to her rooms drunk after a week apart; but she not so sure of him after that --

"Hey Marian, how's yer job going this week"?

"You forgot about me"!

"That's what'a mean, why I'm asking", as Rudi stepped in quietly.

"You got a phone up there. Call next time"!

He also sat quietly. "I call all the time, gal; you ain't never here".

"Maybe that was the message" --

"Come on Marian, we're dancing tonight. Don't get sore with me", folding his feet tidily under the chair. "But I need to eat first. What's in the cooler for us"?

"Only the beers", she said gently. "No food yet".

"Well, what we gonna do? How about pasta; let's go out for some"!

"No; noodles, Chinese; any place on Front Street. Okay".

"Of course we will. You win. Sure". Rudi finally grinned when she sat near to him. He was sometimes a bit expansive with their relations and often pushed an existentialist thing upon her, like the college boys talked of. Yet he was no highbrow; Rudi was a practical man he told everybody and told himself the same.

It was at Marian's place, again, Rudi heard about the road accident. She repeated what Gavin passed on, when Rudi settled at the table with a full plate and drink. He was fully occupied but could listen, as she related the news on her rounds of the sink-fridge-cooker... It was about Wayne, junior member of the work crew and already known in that circle as classic tear-arse, fresh from the town fold and his world by-the-tail. He was nineteen when he hit the tree; out in his first auto when they went off the road at sixty mph and it was late and dark. His best friend was driving the vehicle; but the boys said Wayne was. Anyway, no chance to correct the mistake when three feet from the roadside the large pine tree stood unbending; when their small coup hit the trunk base and sent the radiator over the engine and two boys were slammed into broken metal. Wayne died very quickly; well, he never regained consciousness after the police arrived. His companion was injured for the rest of summer, but went on to live and not tell about it.

Rudi was telephoned: "Can you come to West Side chapel, next Tuesday"?

"What time? Why"?

No one had refused because it was full and interested in the last departing of a young blade, the survey boy who irked everyone with his pranks. A lot of them went to his mother and repeated what she already knew about him. Rudi went up to the mother too, but could not say anything. He was a few important years older, enough to be usually safe in a car at night. But they all had vehicles for work and pleasure and each drove a dangerous course for a few years; so that lady luck had to be with you a long time. Finally Rudi went off, but failed to understand the rationale of the events, not even good horse sense could figure it out for him. He was also shamed with the ignorance: ignorant how a young man would die, ignorant how a mother could listen to the same old rubbish in church -- not helped by what his own mother had to say, when he called at her house for coffee and cake, looking clean and decent with a new kind of quiet --

"Where yuh been Rudi"?

"Church".

"You look great; should go there more often. You might meet a nice girl".

"Not at a funeral" --

"I want to meet the girls you know. When you gonna bring one home so I can talk to her. Your father wants to see one, a decent one".

"What was wrong with Sonia"?

"Your father liked her, all that hair, the hippie girl I suppose"?

"Got any food -- anything left over from dinner I mean"?

One hundred young people each went their own way again at end of day and set to do nothing different the next day. The young never lost their appetite for speed and mistook their lazy thoughts for mourning. But Rudi did keep out of bars that weekend and swam the local pool instead; glad to be young and strong a bit longer and glad he could be sorrowed and sensible at the right time. Wayne was not replaced in the crew that summer, but his name often came up in new arrangements for pairing the crews; how he could be good with maps and such, good as any of his jokes. He was not forgotten that year; but the survey gets through a lot of new blood every season, one way or the other. Rudi saw this whole tragedy through by end of season and was aware how the men always courted danger sooner or later, if the opportunity presented itself; not in a morbid way but with gaiety; a reckless disregard of normal strictures as another kind of fun with a hard edge to it. The final score for them was still more fun than heartache, more laughter than tears at the end. Mirth always won over melancholy, or life over risk; when young men were together in large enough numbers, without women.

Next year, Rudi was assigned far enough north to be put onto a plane; full of woodsmen and roughnecks going into town -- homeward bound from their work contracts out-of-state. Only one empty seat on a small Boeing jet on a Christmas run; when complimentary drinks flowed in the cabin and stewardesses were getting a lot of festive attention. Rudi sat between an Icelandic rock-driller and a half-breed timber choker. But they smelled fresh and hungry for tucker; as four blondes in best mini-skirts repeated their steps up-an-down the aisles with a lot of hot banter and bluff. These girls had to be brave and not squeamish if they were going to work again, after getting their panties yanked down to the knees. Two of them, the others seeming helpless, got their red uniform panties lowered when attending a passenger; the man in the seat behind had an easy task when it came to it. There was more fuss about it later, after the flight, when it got written down and passed around. One of his camp bosses accepted responsibility, with enough lee-way for a one-time only chance; because these men had the best excuses -- hardwork, up-North and Christmas liquor.

Rudi could see the girls were about his age, big pink cheeks and quick blushing young flesh. He enjoyed it all quietly, knowing he would not dare such a deed, but set to tell about it as classic fable from the north. There were lots of quick comments from the passengers, made out loud, meant to be helpful and explanatory --

"That's outrageous, really terrible! What's he drinking"?

"What could happen? He already got fired today"!

"When's the return flight to camp? Get me on it"!

"Thank God for Christmas -- New Year gets even better"!

"Jake obviously needs more drink and less opportunity. He cheats at cards too"!

"Jake thinks he got home already and they overdressed. It's a call for help"!

"It's really a set up -- they got paid for it and the guy is gay"!

Weeks later Rudi was involved with a different kind of woman; she was not blonde and wore no mini-skirt. He was still in town, by January, doing the post season rounds with another happy group. This time with people who also worried about being happy, because they were from college and Rudi came across them when the work season was weeks away. But dark evenings brought young people together again for dancing and drinking. It was a weekend evening and first up to dance gets a lot of attention; the curious attention of a native Indian establishment. His partner was a dwarf lady from the university and he danced with her well enough. So the Indians attending respected him, did not fear him; would leave him alone even though he was a 'Wasp' on reservation property and among Indian gals. Rudi could be daring like that and the full record-play from the music box was his alone. The sitting patrons became an audience of first-timers -- first time to see a midget canoodle on Saturday night, first time in their drinking hole and she a Wasp too. Rudi went round the floor anti-clockwise in a waltz rhythm, which was no trouble to perform; letting him consider his situation and the bigger picture he made that evening: sex among unequals, love amid the enemy, music with the unlikely --

"You got good rhythm, Dorothy; you did this before, yeah"?

"I can easily follow a good lead".

"Brave of you to be straight-up to dance; but you were also quick to drink".

"The real braves are over there, watching us over here"!

"Because they can't do a waltz, or a dipsy waltz. Whoops, here comes the dip"!

"I got it".

"Bet you never thought dancing could be so lonely; could be important and so strange"?

"Can we sit this next one out, please? I need another drink".

"And I want a different tune".

Back to camp Rudi could barely savour the vacation period, before he was over-reacting; a thousand dollars out of pocket and resentful how a good-time was fleeting; how new friends were not to be found up the mountain on a wet night in the cabins. By February his cup was empty again and work had not gotten easier, the days not shorter. His holiday in town had been better than ever; so why did he feel tricked and impoverished. By March, work and confinement together were un-relenting; but one phone-call got through --

"Get back here next weekend Rudi. I got a job for you, I can't do. Can you make Saturday morning"?

"Hi mom".

"You can have your favourite pasta for dinner".

"My weekend-off is next month, the first Saturday. Not till then".

"You tell them I'm sick, or something. Just this once, for me. I can't make it without you Rudi. You're the best thing to happen to me, inspite of your father".

"Alright then, the first Saturday. You gonna get my shell pasta and real peaches sweet from the oven -- all you want this time. Marian wants wine, I said no; but she's a nice girl. She told me about you; I mean you told me about her. That's okay".

"What can I tell my boss"?

"We have to rely on something, someone; both of us".

"Not always" --

45

Driving back towards town he tail-gated an eighteen-wheeler for many miles and every time the truck pulled over he took his cue to eat or drink at new road stops. The driver always sat at the café counter but did not look round, though he must have seen Rudi by then. They continued together like this along inter-state highways; all the way to a turn-off marked as homeward bound. Maybe the man often made friends this way; because his vehicle was very big, powerful and clearly in full control.

CHAPTER FIVE

The British Navy had a warship moored at Fisherman's Wharf for the weekend and open for visitors that Saturday afternoon. A bold sign fastened to the railings, said so. Lots of people were out on a fine day, walking in the sunshine and straying onto the pier beneath some seafood restaurants. The ship was a small destroyer and neatly tied-up alongside a wooden jetty. Its flags were flying and sailors smartly dressed for the show, two of them at the gang-plank ready to assist on-board entry.

But no one was interested, no one went aboard; because the small crowd arriving at the wharf kept walking past the ship. They were more concerned with sea lions at very end of the pier, after hearing them calling and barking in the warm sun. Everyone gathered to watch clumsy creatures splash from the rocks into the water and swim under the pier, like they were hiding or playing. There were calves too, catching the attention of female onlookers and one big bull sat in middle of the herd.

The Captain took this outcome a little hard and started to blow whistles and the lower ranks were lined-up on deck to perform a parade drill. Nothing worked – except an officer finally stepped onto the dockside and waylaid one likely tourist, to talk with him directly. The rest of the crew were glancing at other craft nearby or looking up at the bulk of tourists on a promenade above. But there was still no interest in their ship. The Queen's Royal Navy had been bested by a gang of noisy sea mammals and ignored by a bemused public that day, undisciplined and irreverent.

FIRST STOWAGE

His name is Jim Montpelier, a friend of Rudi Borah, you will know of. In fact they might be half-cousins, or related in some way;

47

but for the thousands of miles between them. One resided in America and Jim always lived in the British Isles; one is a country boy and the other a townie. Jim's hometown was a seaport; a working site with a bit of romantic flavour from the big shipping vessels constructed and supplied from a community of local sea-salts. He wished to tell his own story from early years on the northeast coast; a nowhere place of no import, so as to be good for a boy left alone and free --

It was a good summer, so Jim went into the water every day to swim, to learn how. The sunlight spilled over the waves and across the surface, making the water look playful and friendly. There was a lot of noise at the beach; loads of people playing with balls, floats and water-toys; kids shouting at parents and teens splashing everyone. But it was happy and bright for a young boy, like this, which kept him in good spirits for his special task.

Jim waited till no one was near when he fell forward between the waves and pushed off the bottom, to glide a few feet, face down and straight. He was trying to make like a fish, to be at home in the water and feel free of everything. He also tried to go with the waves. After a swell went past he dived after it to catch the foamy crest, head up and kicking his feet all the way to the shallows. This was best; he seemed to go further and get excited with water filling his ears and thrashing round his head, when the wave finally crashed onto the shore. He resisted playing with friends, because he had to swim, this was his big chance. He seemed to be more grown this year, the way he dedicated himself to the task and saw his opportunity. No one spoke to him, when they must have seen a small boy at the edge of the sea; alone and proud with his quest, very thin and shy. But he kept at it and finally made a few strokes between footfalls on the bottom. He was up and moving on the surface; a big success no one knew about, not even his parents.

However it was a long way off to swim like young men at the rocks. At end of afternoon Jim would sit atop the rocks and watch lean youth dive from small ledges into the dark blue water; then swim-off like a power craft across the surface. He wanted to be like them, brown and strong; brave in the depths and sure of their great swim strokes. They did not see Jim watching, would not care about it, so he could study the models a boy must follow. And there were no girls, no distractions; it appeared to be a masculine imperative they enjoyed in a special way.

His first home was top of a sandy bay by the sea coast. His father toiled at the shipyards, so they had to live close by. Men at the docks worked long hours; or else they were out drinking beer to talk about ships and sea journeys they longed for. Jim was let alone, so he often wandered the coast, sitting upon rock formations to watch the sea lap the shore in a restless pounding; learning how successive tides were continually adding to the drama. He saw how this sea water was alive and strong; beating against a shoreline of sand and stones, cliffs and banks, every day. This was a lot for a young boy; so much to know and understand, such a big world out there and him so small. He tried to face these things squarely and thought to find a place for himself one day; realizing he must prepare for life beyond the horizon he saw and knew that he was not ready. But Jim never did go to sea for work like he thought of; never did sail the far oceans like his father or his father's family. Yet a restless spirit, the yearning for adventure and faraway lands; all these were pounded into his soul, into his small heart; when he spent so much time at the sea-shore, in the water or at the harbour. Not many years later, his father contacted a sea-going master and arranged a passage for him aboard a vessel heading south, after school closed for summer.

First time into London, Jim arrived on a coastal collier, from a coal port in the north. He entered the city by the river, starting from the 'Pool of London' at Tower Bridge, to be guided up-stream by the captain. The old Scotsman knew all about sites to interest a boy and pointed out 'Traitors gate', where the accused left their river ferry to pass through a large wooden gate to be imprisoned and tried for treason; which in Tudor times was the most serious offence landing the most severe punishment. He also pointed out the White Tower, Westminster Parliament and finally the big power station at Battersea.

On the first night their boat moored infront of the river entrance, when Jim was asleep in his berth. Next morning an early sun shone through the porthole and awoke him quickly. He stumbled onto his feet to find his pants and looked out to the day beginning – to see the old bridge before him; two high stone towers and a steel span between them – just like he saw in books, calendars and postcards. This really was London he kept hearing about; with the famous bridge that could lift up in two half's to allow freighters and such go up river. He hurried on deck nearest the galley, to look again, at the bulky structure looming over them amidst the morning light.

"Aye lad, we're waiting for the tide" said the young cook "we should be moving in an hour or so". This was Jim's first voyage on a merchant boat, away from home. He was only a youngster and awed by a historic city and the fabled bridge waiting for them. Jim dressed with the same clothes he always wore, to include a polo-neck sweater, when going ashore to the dock. They were at Battersea a few days to unload coal, then load-up on ballast to go home. Jim could wander the nearby lanes, passing the odours of public houses, much like those in his own town. The shop outlets appeared familiar and the people too; but he thought to stand out, look distinctly different. He was very young but now ready to be a sailor-boy home from the sea in a great city; arriving with new found ship mates and his kit-bag stored on the bunk below. It was a special day for him and he felt sure the whole wide world felt the same way.

The year before, Jim was also a 'skipper', in command of his own sailing craft. When prompted by his mother, he recovered the forgotten model craft from a garden shed and prepared for the season. Jim would hold the yacht under one arm, to carry, marching down to the park to find a small lake. The breeze was already fresh across his face, so he was in a hurry to launch his boat and see it sail across the water, in front of everyone; a bit of a show-off, he needed to see people watching. Jim was proud of the construction his father made and it was big enough to attract a small gathering when he held it at the water's edge; ready to shove-off, after making last minute adjustments to the sails.

"A lovely barque, you got there; what is it" said a man nearby?

"It's a sloop, my father said".

"Your father make it, yes"?

Jim could not explain any more, except to show more pride at that moment. The older man seemed to understand, to keep a respectable distance and go quiet as Jim crouched over and pushed the thing gently; fixing all their attention on the hull creasing through the water, waiting to see a bow wave created. There was lots of luffing of the white sail-cloth and the hull bobbing up-an-down, before enough breeze flowed across the replica deck to make the mast lean over; then it was off and away!

Much later the boy could only stand and stare, when his sailing model gained centre of the pond, becalmed and motionless. The breeze became fickle and spotty, to make for an anxious boy; so he circled the pond's pathway, trying to anticipate where it might go. This uncertain breeze finally deserted them and his yacht stayed out of reach, twisting-an-turning, as if it too was confused and lost in a big park by the sea; as if it was a real boat, trying to reach the open sea a mile or less away. Indeed, the main harbour was just out the park and across the road, where his father worked every day in the dockyards. Jim knew how impressive iron ships were built at this yard and sent out to the North Sea full of freight and laughing men; how steel was strong and heavy, yet floated away like wooden timbers. Both him and his model boat, wished to be free of the pond and set sail on a wide open sea; free of disbelievers and drunkards, toys and kids; out to the deep water heading away from home towards bigger adventures.

'Be careful what you dream about' his father said, 'beware of mermaids and seahorses as figureheads on the horizon'. Jim stood at the rail amidships, recalling his father's mocking sense and looked across the empty sea, which was by then flat and calm. He was only thirteen years old, so could be reckless and bold sometimes. He leaned over the blackened hulk and reached down, holding on with

51

the other hand. He kept reaching, stretching down to touch the water's surface and trail his fingers in the sea for a few minutes. It was thin and cold, splashing over his hand; while he tried to understand how it would become rough and stormy without warning, angry and cruel. No one else was up on deck; the captain and crew busy at routine schedules to forget about a boy on their boat.

It was mid-day and lunch was over. Jim helped in the galley and when everything went quiet he went off alone, going to the focsul to look ahead; to see the direction they headed and stopped midway on the lower gangway which surrounded the two cargo holds. It was always dirty and rusty, neglected, so he avoided touching anything. He was gazing at the surrounding sea so very close at midships and it exerted a strong attraction; to draw him under its spell and distract with a massive presence. He was close enough to watch foaming action on the surface where the hull disturbed the water, close enough to look into a few feet of sea-water beneath him. Holding the water in his hand, it was colourless and transparent; but away from the side it was green, dark green/blue, like a large mass of dirty bath water.

Jim eventually withdrew his hand and stood up, stepped back from the siding. He knew the captain might be afraid for his safety to see this and he only a boy, who had to please the adults in his life and his parents too, who sent him out there. The weather was holding, fine and bright, to make him restless and impatient; but he still very young, which meant confusion because he was alone without guidance. He spent a lot of time on his own, like this, when the crew went off to their watch duty with the engines or up to the bridge compartment. Though he was not lonely or sad. In fact Jim was glad to be out on a collier that summer, far away from family and home, way out upon the high seas.

It was exciting for a boy to be moving like this, like his father talked of; cruising slowly all day and right through the night. He also knew the deep sea was dangerous; how their craft was small and vulnerable. Scary too, the way it sat so low in the water to roll with the ocean swell; the dirty old engine puffing away in the smoke stack and noisy seagulls following, watching from above.

Jim remembered how his father was sent to work by the time he was fourteen; starting in the same shipyards which produced the craft Jim now sailed in. He heard all about the life of sailors; foreign lands across the ocean and how boats were beautiful, even rusty old coal carriers. 'Why Captain Cook himself' his father said, 'used our local colliers to discover Australia, back in Seventeen-eighty-eight! Aye, they served him well' when they were at breakfast one day.

By the third day, Jim found himself a job, an important task on his first voyage no one else wanted. He became tea-boy to the wheel house. He took hot tea from the galley up to the captain and first-officer. It was a daring task, fetching a handful of empty mugs back to the galley and taking fresh brew the other way; when he must hold onto the well-worn rails up steep metal steps, with one hand, while the ship always seemed to roll more at this time. The door at the top was heavy on its hinges, with a high safety step at the entrance, he never got used to. But the bridge crew were pleased to see the new cabin boy at his chore, because they always wanted a hot drink, specially at evening. Jim saw them pouring over the sea charts on a raised table or sweeping the far horizon with heavy black binoculars. A dull voice on the radio detailed weather conditions, over and over. On top of this, a brisk exchange was going on between the first-mate and another ship nearby, on the same radio system; making for a lot of conflicting talk.

The engine crew also wanted tea and were not shy to say so. Jim descended into a cavernous chamber of strange odours and mechanical noises; the whole place throbbed and vibrated from the big drive shaft. It was also warm and dark, where two men in coveralls smoked cigarettes as they gazed up at dials, knobs and gauges; a bit frightening for Jim like being in the belly of a great whale diving to the depths. They enjoyed Jim's service but said little in return, intent on the engine readings and did not encourage him to stay below, as if ashamed of their work. It was dirty duty; grimy stains on their overalls, with dirty oil on every flat surface and their hands blackened. Conversation was short along with nods and hand-signals; not meant as rudeness but clearly appropriate in the circumstance. Yet these same engineers were very talkative up top in the galley and took more drink, than anyone else in the pubs, when they got ashore.

MV Glenside was in the great tradition of coastal colliers used for Captain Cook's world voyages. But Jim's vessel was ugly, unlike Cook's sailing ships. It was like a bucket with an engine at the rear, a coal bucket. The main structure served as the hold with a wheel house sighted above the engines. Forward was anchor stowage and a small prow of no consequence. She also needed some kind of cargo for ballast, to keep the craft stable – going south with the coal and coming back carrying stone chips. Jim recalled how good his boat looked at the dockside; an impressive round hull, tied with heavy ropes, completely filling one side of the dock. He could see ladders going up to the bridge and railings round the back, like it was a house. A black funnel rose behind the lifeboats and was blasting out blue smoke, while he stood there. Jim was justly keen and secure with such a construction for any sea, in any weather. But when they got away from port, out beyond land sightings, it became a very small craft for him. When the sea rose up ahead of them, the prow did not lift up and for a long time their boat was swallowed by the swell, hidden from view. It seemed like a mere matchstick adrift on the sea, making no headway and waiting to founder. But Jim could not say so; he never talked like this to anyone, because the crew never said anything was wrong.

Before he went to bed, the captain took him aside one evening and pressed a book into his hand: Stevenson's 'Kidnapped'. It was a worn copy but good enough to read and keep safe – "Here lad, this story is for you and covers the same seas we navigate. Take it to your cabin and have a good read".

"Thankyou Sir, I will" and Jim clasped it to his chest to descend the steps below. The first night he looked for illustrations and read the last pages – to see how Davy Balfour fared at the end. The captain did not enquire about the book any further, until it was passed back at journey's end, when Jim made some brief comments upon the story. Both agreed it worthwhile material for anyone who sailed the North Sea; the captain enjoyed a Scottish story and Master Balfour was the same age as Jim. Without reading at night, it still took no time before sleeping. When you lay flat in the dark, the continuous motion of the vessel eliminated worries and cares; dreams and wishes became as one very quickly, for pleasant slumber. It was the same every night, until the boat docked; when Jim's cabin mate returned from the pub ashore full of beer and began banging round the cabin. It was so loud and violent that Jim believed the man was fighting with someone. When it happened again the next two nights, he realized it was not really a violent outbreak, more like his father falling over the furniture at home. Next morning Jim was hoping the man would say something, but he was already gone, to his shipboard duty at the cargo. This crew member was acting as bosun and directing the unloading of coal for the power station. A worthwhile task, Jim thought, worthy of respect and admiration; because it was a rough/dirty job, but very necessary as any boy could see. Meanwhile, the cook's duties were more familiar, more accommodating. Jim would rush to the galley thinking his friend was inside, usually ready to talk and listen; because he was young too, a mere sixteen just out of school. The pots and pans were sliding across the stove banging into metal guards and the cooking utensils hanging above were crashing into each other as they swayed to the boats heaving – like the cook was present and working to prepare the food. But the lad was not there – only the sounds of cooking and warm smells wafting out the doorway. Jim sat at the table anyway and looked to the playing cards sitting at the corner, to the pots boiling and steaming away; waiting for someone to show, so they would sit beside him.

Going north on the return journey, the ship was bound for Scotland, a fishing town on way to Inverness. They were contracted to take a load of granite chips for the home port, between coal shipments. The Glenside reached the small port of Buckie in late morning, so Jim thought to go ashore after eating lunch in the galley. Two of the deck-hands scrambled ashore to tie mooring lines to bollards on the dock, painted tar-black and looking very sturdy. It was fresh, breezy weather, making Jim restless again and ready to be the first crew member into town. But he began by sitting with three of the crew in their galley, to eat baked-beans on toast with a mug of sweet tea; a favoured dish for lowly seamen, like they were at home in the kitchen with a kindly woman in attendance. There was usually a warm feeling when any of the men sat together to eat and talk, which would usually make Jim linger at the table.

"Away you go lad and don't get lost; because we can't go looking for you. Avoid them pubs and get back before dark"!

"Alright, I will" – he not knowing what to say.

"Come back an-tell us what you find ashore, don't forget your shipmates".

Jim found a woollen garment to pull over his head; it was off-white with a polo neck, made to look like submariner's clothing. He was thankful for this item his father gave; to get him ready for the world as young cabin boy from a working collier, in a tiny Scottish town. He felt people must be watching him, taking notice of a daring boy entering a foreign country, with only a hand-me-down sweater to protect him. Jim easily found his way from the dock, because he was becoming a junior sea-salt; stepping up some slopping concrete to find the first roadway and took a right turn. He was returning from his voyage and wanted towns-people to see how he was safe and well; like a hunter home from the hill, or soldier returned from the wars --

The road going right took a turn up a hill and Jim fell into step for it. He was striding past terraced houses overlooking the small bay and saw women on the pavement, a line of them up the street. They were all on hands-an-knees washing the stone flagging with soap and water. He was really amazed to see young women scrubbing away with hand brushes; obviously young wives from the homes adjacent, fussy and diligent. They did not look up at the boy, but must have seen him going onto the road to avoid stepping into their soapy water. Jim was young and proud, but they were more proud and less vague, more useful and less free. He could think that women were important too, not just the sea-salts and they were practical, if not recognized as such. He was to be duly humbled; these land-lubbers had bested him and females at that; they dealt his ideals and his dreams a tempering blow that day.

Reaching the top of his hill Jim continued walking down the other side feeling a little chastened, a little out of breath. There was lots of traffic round a central junction, shop fronts and busy people – what he came to expect in any town. He followed his nose to a post-office store and bought a card to send home. It was a brown-an-white photo of Buckie harbour with slopes behind and in the foreground fishing boats waited at anchor lines. He wrote on the back and asked the store lady for a stamp: "Hello mother/father – I am in Scotland today. Last week I was sea-sick; now trying to get my sea-legs. Tomorrow we are going to Seaham to unload the stone chips we got today; but I like to go to London with the coal. Love from Jim". He was trying to be fair with his parents; not to be sentimental for his father, yet mindful of a young mother at home.

Little did Jim know that many more journeys were to come for him, but not always across the sea. Some of these travels would last for months or years and with no return, no going back. Oceans and harbours and were often warmer elsewhere, quite different; boats would be clean and sleek, like the schooners from America. Was he attempting to leave something behind, like this, or was he truly venturing to seek and learn? These sorts of troubles, thoughts, followed him all the way along his long walk from town. Seems there was more to travel than just leaving home, lots of places out there to know about, new people and happy surprises waiting for him. Buckie and the Glenside were a good start for the fretful boy, who retraced his steps back to the ship's berth; looking upwards this time at the seagulls circling and white clouds building. Jim was asking questions, all kinds of questions about himself and the things he found.

CHAPTER SIX

A man in a tan business suit suddenly appeared from the tables at front with a golden trumpet and joined onto the group of musicians already playing. It was late on Friday evening, in a popular café-bar with lots of oddities gathered to eat, drink and talk. He took centre stage and blew hard; stretching his instrument way out in front of him to take the lead, like it was a gala occasion. It was Jazz mostly and some popular tunes we all heard from TV or the movies. But the crowd loved it, because he was really state's attorney for the district and not a café performer. Obviously, he played like this at college and school before that; long before he came to be a lawyer in town. Everyone loved the idea of music coming from a public official -- great sounds, plaintive and strong, from their prosecutor that night. It was an unexpected treat for all to hear and see, confusing and exciting. This strange mix of law with music, made for a lot of attention and he kept blowing at his shiny horn, right on till the midnight hour. Outside it was still dark and cool, inside it was now hot and loud.

MINOR CHARACTERS

There's a lot to learn, it takes years to find your way in the world, Rudi would consider in an idle moment; walking the dog or driving at night, alone and unprotected. He also knew how many boys did not find the same and married the first gal they knew; grabbed any job out of school and took a house near home and parents. It seemed to be simple for them, from Rudi's view-point, as if life was pre-ordained. Maybe Rudi was just restless, like his own father and tried to justify his wanderings, his vagrancies and his dreaming. Work was his first adventure after school; he took it seriously straight away and knew it was important for a long time to come, like the rest of his family. His father and grandfather had little schooling and long hours of employment. Of course it was the men Rudi was thinking about and man's work, like farming --

"There you are Rudi; don't spend it all at once, don't lose it", the small-holder added when he handed out the wages to two men and a boy. It was a small place up the valley, with mixed enterprises of milking cows, pigs and hens; with corn and wheat at harvest time – enough work for them all year round.

"Don't spend it on the ladies" Cliff said. He was the younger man but also the more worldly, the man with ready stories and earthy advice.

"And not on drink" came from the older one.

They knew it was a first time for Rudi and enjoyed teasing a youngster at Friday afternoon paytime. Rudi could not reply, he could only fumble with the small brown envelope and found a front pocket empty. 'Don't lose it', he seemed to hear again and shoved his hand inside, to push the thing deep down against his leg. But it was time to go; stepping smartly towards his bike to mount, like it was a horse out on the range, then ride off straight like a soldier on parade. He was full of pride and reserve as he headed towards the main gate on the road; at the same time feeling they were watching, trying to laugh about him one more time. It had been a fine day; some evening light and a soft breeze reaching his face, as he continued to the gate and turned left up the hill towards his lodgings.

By then Cliff and the other man had ridden alongside on their own bikes and before they turned right at the gate, Cliff said: "funny thing, we all leave together, for the first and last time. I'm quitting today, to go trucking".

"Goodnight lad and good luck to you" said the other man!

"Goodnight" chimed-in Rudi.

Rudi had the pay-packet deep in his pocket, but not deep enough to forget, so he had to stop. Only a few yards up the hill, he got off his bike and laid it against the hedge; an unbroken section where he could crawl under and rest against the fence behind. Then he fished

60

out the packet from his pants and tore open the top. Inside was a paper docket and folded behind were new bank notes, with some coins at the bottom. It was an exciting package, not unlike a Christmas surprise at home; his very first pay for a real job, real man's work away from hearth and home, out in the big wide world. The paper info was an account of hours he worked and the overtime; with a column for taxes, deductions and final amount. He hurried over it and put to one side, then began unfolding the notes and counting the coins. Yes, it was all there, as the docket said. But he kept counting and feeling the crisp notes with his soiled fingers, looking at them as his father would at home infront of his mother. The weeks of hard work melted away, because he was actually paid real money; so that all the dirt and grime, the awkwardness and discomfort, long hours and stale food, did not matter anymore. He forgot about it very quickly, sitting under the hedge, fondling his remittance payment in a secret hideaway. The money made everything alright, made his venture a success and worth continuing; school did not matter anymore, nor his town neighbours or his friends, not even his own family at that moment. Though he continued like this for several months, it was the first week he remembered; the first full amount of wages and how it felt to earn money like any other men. When he finally left the holding, he had saved enough to purchase his first automobile. It was nothing new, but he wanted to taste the freedom of the road; in an old Ford cruiser with two-tone colours and lots of chrome at the front. Clearly it was out-dated, but the sales lot claimed it to be in cherry condition; so he set to develop some pride in the vehicle and took no mind of the teasing he got.

The first real journey he had was over to the coast for an unspecified vacation. He was drawing directly on his savings, but did not worry; because he was ready to work again when the time came. One afternoon he sat in a café with a new found friend; an unlikely pal for a young country boy.

"This town is dead" Tom said; "yes it is, the place is really dead"!

61

He was an old man and could get away with such boldness. He could also get away with saying outrageous things to young ladies, like "I'm going to fly you up to the moon, young Miss, yes I am". But the girl was only small, about eight years old.

Rudi was with Tom a lot by then; trying to be helpful and learn about California from his friend, who was here since the 'year of the quake' in 1906. He took Tom over to a park at the town center, to cut his finger nails which were very old and very hard. Sometimes he cut his toe nails if they could sit on the grass and Tom pressed Rudi with five dollars for some gas in the car.

Rudi was now friends with the little girl, because she really was a stunning little creature, with blond hair and wonderful round eyes. But she was very shy to talk, except she kept looking at Rudi and stuck out her tummy for pride. It seems Tom had directed him onto the little mite in a surprising way. In fact Rudi had to make friends with the girl's parents too, not much older than himself. They would sit together in a popular cafe of the town and tease her about Rudi and about Tom.

Tom also liked to ride in the car when Rudi had to travel for an errand or visit someone out of town. He would sit in the front and ignore the driving, talking about California and when he lived in Los Angeles with famous writers like Raymond Chandler and Scott Fitzgerald. "Scott was a crazy son-ofa-gun; he got the most money for a story and spent it on booze and the track"! It seems that Tom was not like this, yet showed keen interest in his rival. "I went drinking with Chandler once, in a terrible barrio, but he was paying".

The car was long and heavy, with big bench seats front-an-back, so as to make a comfortable ride across town and along the beach road. The open window let in salty spray from the sea and special beach aromas of sun cream and kelp mixed together. He drove slow as possible and let Tom comment on the scenes and people they saw, which in some way connected with his own youth years ago in LA.

Back into town Rudi looked out for the girl; he developed a fascination with her and tried hard to be friends. Tom had forgotten, he never mentioned her again. Now it was Rudi's turn to make the little girl talk or react; to break through the silence, her shyness. The parents were keen on this too.

"Come on Nancy, talk to your friend, don't you like him" made her more resistant!

This went on for weeks, whenever they met-up at the café, but no change. Then one day they all went out the cafe to find the green park Tom enjoyed and sat together on the thick lawn grass, talking about the new music scene and college courses. They were sitting amid buttercups and small white daisies and Rudi was picking the daisies. Eventually he made a necklace from them, by joining the stems, like he learned as a boy at home. He placed this over the girl's head and let it rest upon her shoulders. It seemed to work well and held together, looking bright and fresh. The girl was still silent but kept looking at it upon her chest. She did not try to take it off or touch with her fingers, but pushed out her chest like before, with a lot of pride.

"I think she likes it" the father said, "yes she does".

"Say thankyou, sweetheart" said the mother.

It appeared she did like the necklace and got up to walk round, to show everyone what she had. Her blue eyes shone brightly and opened wider. She went over to where Rudi sat and picked up his hand to hold tightly for a few minutes. Her parents were following all this intently and trying to keep quiet. This was their first child and her silences were carefully followed the same as her bright chatter. To confirm their special interest, they needed to get her lots of attention, even from near strangers. Rudi enjoyed his part, but needed to meet more gals and venture out at evening. Matt was a lot younger than Tom and less likely to befriend children. He was putting-up half the gas money for their night out; he made the phone calls and picked out the movie.

"Let's go Rudi, it's late"!

"Okay Matthew – I like western movies". And the two young men got over to the cinema line to meet-up with more friends and two gals from the valley unknown to Rudy or Matt. It was Saturday evening, a special time for young people in California and either it was a dance hall outing or a cinema show every weekend – so the boys could kick over the traces and be set free. No doubt the gals had other reasons for showing at the picture house. Maybe they were sweet on Clark Gable, or wanted to watch Marilyn Monroe as beauty queen of America, see how to get more attention from the boys.

"Good evening boys, evening girls" Rudi said, turning round politely to include everyone in his gaze. He saw enough to notice a blonde gal with boots and pony tail, the other female more slight and bookish with glasses and cardigan; a bit of a mis-matched pair he thought. As the line towards the entrance moved forward, the group arranged themselves into pairs, so they could be seated better. Everyone was talking, happy to be out and entertained for an evening. It was the big movie of the year for college kids: 'The Misfits' by Arthur Miller and everyone knew how he was married to Marilyn and wrote the script especially for her.

Rudi was in an aisle seat with his feet sticking out, for comfort and convenience; like a lonesome cowboy, he thought of. He was beside Matt and behind the girls; the other boys on his left side in the same row. But everyone had someone to talk to, listen to. He saw it was a black-an-white production, not really like 'Film Noir' from the Nineteen-forties, or like a B-movie. It wasn't really a western either, with scenes from Reno-Nevada, horses and aircraft and the opening narrative was about divorce; women disembarking from the trail bus to file for legal separation. In fact, Rudi was struggling with the story idea; so many conflicting themes and people, to make it difficult to follow. He would only mumble in reply to his pal's comments, affecting a distracted appearance instead of confusion like he really felt. Still, it was intriguing for him; the bare-faced café scene near the beginning and Monty Clift on the telephone to his mother like he was in a war-zone. Clark Gable seemed to be the central character, but not a hero like a western movie, more like a protagonist or narrator. There was no main character because everyone had a lot to say; even the minor characters liked the camera and hogged centre stage sometimes. Rudi liked to watch Monty after he made the phone-call to his mother, wearing big white bandages round his head under a handsome white stetson. Nothing he said made any sense, yet it all sounded so beautiful and a bit heroic. Rudi got the meaning from inferences or responses and all the images lined-up in a modern desert landscape. The movement and time-of-day ran ahead of the characters, to compel sympathy and attention from the audience, even if they did not understand or comprehend anything.

Girls and young ladies were always in the bigger picture, for young men. Matthew was a little more proactive than Rudi, maybe more honest. He got them over to the 'Blue Light' club, to see more girls and fewer clothes. It was the late-nite club in town, where gals shed their garments and their inhibitions for sad and lonely men. But Rudi was neither, he was simply curious and liked to please Matt like this, specially on the weekends. For a few hours on Friday-nite, these gals were not lurking in the background anymore; the business of sex-appeal was up-front and centre. Zygotes and hormones were unleashed and upgraded, to confirm youth and energy with the men, allure and attention for the gals.

'Boy she is amazing, sexy and alluring', Rudi mused as he crouched in his seat at one side of the round platform stage, centered in the bar-room off Front Street. Rudi had parked his sedan at the rear and sneaked into a side door to avoid notice, because it was his home town. She was an unknown mix of Asian stock, she admitted one time, after he sported her a large orange drink between dance routines in her break.

He was smitten with this stripper, but it was also useless; because she went with biker boys and was escorted by bouncers every night as if she worried about the admirers. He was at a clear disadvantage, he knew this; but hoping for a lucky opening in her presentation, in her countenance. But he never found this; though he went to see her every Friday evening and took her a bottle of home-made hooch and some flowers he stole from a gravesite – nothing worked. Nothing to notice him, set him above the rest – until she got angry one night, when Rudi claimed she overcharged him; one hundred dollars taken off his credit card. He went to the bar manager to politely enquire about an error on the tab and she was telephoned; to appear fifteen minutes later, on her night off, looking quite different. She wore a dark-brown beret on her head and modest-style jacket on top of casual pants – like a college girl in the park. But Buffy was no college gal, like that; she was tough and quick; bristling infront of him and full of tough repartee. She was smart like a college co-ed, but it was 'street smarts' with a double-edged tongue. The girl finally noticed him alright, though not in the way he hoped for --

"I did not cheat you"!

"No, never said that, it was just a mistake".

"Get me another orange" she asked the waitress hovering nearby.

"Me too" he said, "without the ice, please". Strangely this last request peaked her interest, looking round to the other girl to see her response, they both expired together in frustration. Rudi was standing out by now, uniquely, as a man requiring respect; he was discerning and stubborn with it. But all the staff were now looking his way; he was out-numbered with no chance to win anything. They would be enjoying the human comedy – to watch him as clumsy clown in the ring, stumbling over the main attraction, their show lady. The girl herself had now taken better interest in Rudi, but it was too late to change track. Prudence and caution dictated he withdraw while he still had his dignity and his credit.

Because Rudi left his number at the bar, a few days later he got a message on his phone; but there was no content, just a lot of background noise and a woman saying, 'hello, hello'. He got another like message a week later, but no return number. It sounded like a young voice, interested in reaching him. It was all too late now and clearly a bit risky for a country-style boy to seek any kind of liaison in club premises; regarded as off-limits for most people. He had gotten into the wrong kind of horse race and was making too free with his money. Even Matt stayed away, guilty with his involvement;

a simple diversion for them had blown-up into a bit of a sore issue, troubling and regrettable.

A few weeks later Matthew came up with a better idea; two weeks in Mexico at a fishing town, where blue marlin were hunted for sporting prowess and restaurants served every kind of bean you could think of. It wasn't the US any more, for sure; not always safe and often very strange for Americans. The first day they went out in red-plastic kayaks, to look for whales and bat fish. Matt said if there was no wind to slow them, they would stop at Santa Maria bay, to snorkel and swim for the small coloured fish on the coral. He was in his element, enjoyed talking about everything; knowing Rudi was new to Mexico and the Sea of Cortez --

"Look a bat fish, see it"?

"What"!

"A manta ray, but we say 'bat fish'".

"Yeah, I can see why". A few feet on the left a large dark shadow broke the surface and flapped its wings like a bird; maybe three feet across and no mistaking a singular creature, swimming slowly for Rudi to see.

"Keep going, there's more! The hump-back whales are here this month, to feed and mate, before heading back to Alaska. Follow me"!

The two men returned to a purposeful paddle stroke, one behind the other and headed towards a rocky point where two bigger boats were positioned together. These craft were full of tourists, crowding one side of the deck, with cameras and binoculars. There was a lot of happy excitement and focus on the water ahead. Rudi understood it meant something worthwhile to see and pulled harder on the paddles behind Matt. Between the two boats, whales were playing at the surface and looked like two adults with two calves; rolling in the swell and lifting their heads out the water, raising a tail or flipper up high for everyone to see. The women on the boats were squealing out loud with Matt hiding his expression behind sunglasses. Rudi positioned his craft alongside and let it all happen right infront of

67

them, without talking and without any camera. For about an hour the four whales played-up for the visitors, breaching then sinking under the hulls, rolling round and splashing – knowing how to put on a good show. Mexico turned out alright for the Yankee boys, because they did not outstay their welcome and spent enough dollars to be friendly --

The next adventure for Rudi was in a different direction and he was on his own this time. Matt was a good companion and long-time friend, but didn't like the north or the cold. After their visit to the Baja, he went home to California to tell his tall tales to the unlikely, anyone who would listen. Being very young Rudi was still restless and curious; so not long before he left home again, to try something not even his father tried. Before summer ended he got a rail ticket, leaving his automobile safely in the garage next to his father's. The nights were cooling quickly, but daytime sun held the ice and snow at bay; it was some time before the big freeze and allowed a young man free passage into a remote hinterland --

Rudi went on the train, going north to the Artic; sitting on the window seat trying to discern what he saw of the boreal forest; thousands of lakes either side of the rail tracks and a lone moose standing in the wet rushes. It also appeared threatening when he would see no sign of people or settlements for days, when he usually enjoyed wide open territory. This land was very empty – only the big sky over endless flatlands, water and greenery, weather and wind. Mile after mile like this -- an extensive terrain beneath the biggest sky and not in the background this time but up-front in the foreground. He could not see any living creatures and no human life; just a full force of raw elements across the land, with no fences, no boundaries and no restraint.

Inside the carriage there were people: Canadians and native Indians. He thought of Northern Cree Indians he heard about, very tall and reserved. One of them sat opposite him and slept there at night; she was also tall and quiet. The girl was very striking, good looking and shy; so Rudi had to speak and find out more. "What's your name" and "where you going" -- got a clear answer but the following questions were not accepted the same, when she turned to the window and fixed her gaze away. He then started talking about himself and included outlandish opinions to keep her interested. He became unusually loquacious to try hold her attention and said things he should not have – like jokes about Eskimos and romance, lies about his preferences and dislikes, embellishments and hyperbole...

"My name is Rudi, short for Rudolph from my grandfather's side; he was German stock and my mother of mixed blood from Dakota. But I lived in California, outside of Fresno, where William Saroyan lived. D'you know they have a theatre there now, named after him? I don't like plays myself and the kind of folk they attract, with the weird clothes and a lot of self-conscious talk. I much prefer his short stories, about ordinary people in California. Well they don't come across as ordinary, but they are real and humorous. I just can't stand people who won't/can't, laugh at themselves"...

This went on for three days-an-nights and the girl responded occasionally, when an answer was obvious and short; otherwise she regarded him as a threat because of what she heard, regarding talkative whites and young men. But it was a train, so no escape for her; except she walk down the aisle to find a washroom or go to the dining car at meal-times. For Rudi she was of real interest, to counter the overwhelming wilderness which surrounded them. He needed assurance from a human voice and liked a young female who showed sweetness and promise; in a land that was cold and hard, big and unfeeling. He knew the gal would not understand this and would consider him quite differently. For all her youth and beauty she was also remote and unreachable like aurora borealis in the sky, like polar-bear cubs on the ice, or Eskimo gals off the tundra. In fact she was Eskimo, he heard later, not Cree Indian.

On the way back, Rudi was full of thoughts about what he saw in the north and the people in a tiny settlement without office blocks, neon stuff or traffic. Such places were so different to what he knew and the residents almost foreign to him. When he sat at his window seat again, he gazed at the same vacant scenes; trying to make connections, to understand his country and where he might fit in. How far away need he go, before he could find a place in the scheme of things, like his father said? Should he ever figure this out and would he be ready?

CHAPTER SEVEN

He sat on a soft chair opposite the bed and started to read, anything; a magazine, old newspaper, a Readers digest; flicking through the pages and keeping his gaze down. She was a very old lady dozing off and not paying him a lot of attention; at the same time needing a visitor by this time of day, late afternoon. He also looked out the window, to watch birds flying across the blue sky or see branches of a tree moving in the wind; because there was nothing moving inside the room. Only the lady's chest moved, ever so little, up and down in feint breaths; if he looked hard enough. It was like this the next day and same for the following week; while the man distracted his attention outside, or onto some reading he found on the tables. It was a quiet business, as if nothing was really happening for them. But something very serious was happening; a long life was coming to an end, slowly and peacefully.

SOLDIER'S HOME

Going home is a return, going back to a familiar place, where you were known as a decent sort of ordinary guy. It happens after work, or college, or some time overseas. This may be a welcome return for a lot of people and for some it is not going backwards, it is going forwards. When Rudi came into town it rained, like the day he left; spring rain which came with cloudy sunshine, not to spoil anything. Rudi was not upset with this, or with coming home again. He walked at an even pace from the bus stand, with two travel bags; past the same stores, homes, schools and wanted to be the same himself; but it was not possible. A step through the door of his home, his father's home, was reassuring and stale at the same time; for the next week he enjoyed re-discovering his room and the possessions left there. Because it was April he had winter and summer together for a while and got out his rifle one day, his hunting weapon, to lay on the bed;

71

though he did not clean it or check the action. He also got out two books he knew in the room and opened them each night to read before sleep, yet he could only thumb the pages and smoke a small cigar late at night. He smoked more than he read, reclining in his room or comfortable out in the garden furniture. But he was only average student in High School, so why did he think to read now, after the war.

After two weeks like this his father had a talk with him at the table during dinner, about going to college, the junior college; how he could stay at home to study and use the second family car. He could date girls with the car because he was back from the military and his father knew about that – World War Two and his return home to no job, no money and no gal. His father was good about it when Rudi said little in reply, except his head fell forward in some kind of shame. When Rudi only listened, his father was cool and left him seated; he backed off and began something else. But his step-mother wanted Rudi to talk; wanted him not only to agree but promise and obey. She went on about the college and a job untill Rudi had to leave and go into the garden to smoke again. He had no answers; it was not insolence or disrespect, it was fatigue and isolation --

"Listen, you must work Rudi. It's been three weeks. Get any job, you hear", as she approached his bedroom door. "Go into town tomorrow, first thing and talk to someone"!

"Who", he tried to reply, "where"?

"Our county bank, the mail office, lots of places" -- she was now occupying the doorway. "Why not try the employment agents; we know Mister Wheldon".

"You mean the fields again"?

"No something better, something more", she still standing firmly. "He knows you came home, after three years. We told him about it".

"Who else you told"?

A few minutes more of this and Rudi had to move; even if laying on his bed trying to relax. He had to escape away, this time into town, landing on the library steps; the main library entrance, without a smoke or small change for the café. It was afternoon when school came out and some of the girls went straight to the library for books for school. He recognized letter-jackets of the senior year and types he knew five years ago when he was a senior football letter. They arrived in pairs or threes with school bags and lots of quick chat. He could see their teeth-braces and the slim-belted waists of girls between fifteen and eighteen years because they did not see him on the steps. Rudi could not date these girls now, not even if he got the second car out. But he wanted to see them again the next day; sit the same place quietly and wish there'd been no war and he not left home or left the town. He did this for three days in a row; till he thought they may realize he was looking at them and become alarmed. Then he sat somewhere else that week, at the bus-station in the mornings or the river at night. He walked from home to the river, or to the bus depot; but when he went to the agency to see about a job, he drove the station-wagon and parked on the main street to arrive in jacket and shoes. At other times he enjoyed a hunting coat he always used with pants from the service, low-top boots and belt; so's he would fit in with the town citizens, thinking to look like one of them – but not today.

"Glad to see you Rudi. Come on in". Mr. Wheldon was serious and expansive. "How are you these days? Please seat yourself", as he moved opposite to another chair.

"Just fine" --

"Your mother says you'd like a job – yes! You need to work, don't you"? He still was not smiling.

"Thanks for seeing me".

"You homesick all that time away; she said you missed us. Now you're back -- right"!

"Yes".

A folder of papers was between them and Rudi began to scribble in the blanks; all kinds of information forms in different shades of colour. This took about thirty minutes of empty silence while Mr. Wheldon went out to another office room. On his return he used the telephone twice, including Rudi's name in the hearty chat.

"Well, come round again next week. Okay", quickly getting back to his feet.

"The fields, I don't mind; not really. Not like what I said".

"No, Rudi; nothing with farmers or their produce. We're going to find you something different this time".

"Alright".

"Say hello to your father; I haven't spoken to him in awhile. And here, take these. I was going to throw them away. Maybe you'd like them"? Mr. Wheldon piled about a dozen magazines onto Rudi's arms; then took him to the front entrance as he began grinning for some unknown reason.

"Thankyou Mister Wheldon". Before he could see what they were, Rudi got into his auto and let the magazines fall onto the passenger seat.

"Ask your father to call me", Mr. Wheldon finally beaming and waving. "So long Rudi and good luck to you. Yeah"!

They were photo magazines, he realized; some of them 'Playboy', some 'National Geographic' and 'Popular Mechanics'. But it was the 'Playboys' Rudi saw first as he headed back home, driving cautiously on a slow-way route to the house. Taking them home he had to decide if he was to tell his father and did he really have to hide them from his step-mother. He put them on the centre table in his room, with the back-covers upwards and an alarm clock on top, to peruse later after the dinner. He wanted to see American girls looking good and try to find them attractive, after so long away; to find them appealing as Asian girls. He would read through late each night and see pictures of girls in cars, in a house or a swimming pool and enjoy the joke stories about them. But it was difficult to do this, to make it a pleasure and not worry about how all the girls seemed to be blonde, how the men looked so happy and popular. He was hoping to find the girls attractive but could not hope to be like the men again. A story about the war caught his attention and he followed it without thinking, needing to read something about what he already knew.

74

By June he found it warm and lazy so continued on his walks, or smoking at his favourite places this side of town. Every day seemed much the same; then one Saturday a girl came to see him --

"Hi Rudi, what you doing today"?

"Hey there – nothing much. Come here"! He put out a hand as he turned in his desk chair away from the window view, to see a girl of ten years with real blonde hair and summer shirt. She was shy but came into his room, as always, after getting away from her mother down-stairs.

"What's this", she folded over a magazine on the table because the strong colours caught her attention.

"I was just reading, that's all".

"But it's all pictures – no words"!

"Yeah, lots of words inside, to read", not getting further than the cover-photo of a motor-cycle she arrived at his desk.

"Now I'm writing a letter to my mother – your grandmother I mean".

"Can I see"?

"Yes and you can speak as well".

"What"?

"I mean to your grandma; you can write some words to her, here".

"Don't know what to say" --

They went out the room and joined the girl's mother, who was also Rudi's sister and chattered across the kitchen table. Rudi mentioned a couple of errands and taking the girl along. They began with a casual walk down the street because it was early; going anywhere because Rudi was the girl's favourite uncle and good escape from her own mother. While the two mothers sat in a kitchen catching up on the week, the two friends had a different idea of Saturday; escaping or beginning the week not ending it. Rudi had no grown-up responsibilities yet and was still free like his small companion – like spring was between winter and summer, Rudi was between youth and full adult. The child could not know this and went to Rudi's room every time her mother let her go; she would reach out to him because he was young like her and not for long.

Back to his room Rudi found his rifle again, an old-style lever action and finally dusted the stock and barrel before standing it behind the window curtains. He looked at his books on the wall shelves but did not pull any out; just tilted one or two forward to see the title and moved along. A 'Selection of Robert Frost' with sketches of New England was now falling to bits; next were more poems from Britain and Leonard Cohen in Canada. The shelf above had gift books like 'Hiawatha' off his grandfather, 'Dylan Thomas' from an Army friend, some anthropology and a 'King James' bible from elder family. He saw these books each morning from his bed, to check they were still there, when he might want to take one and open and use. Their presence was definitive and collective, so Rudi could not part with any, even if he did not read them that summer. In the army he craved movies, Hollywood stuff not books and viewed them in the company mess. Solitary pursuits and reading were ill-considered in the service.

That afternoon he was still not reading but solitary, because the militia did not prepare you for leaving, just as he was not prepared to join-up. His jackets and coats, ties and shirts, were under plastic covers in the closet made-over by his step-mother. His personal items were hidden away in drawers and his letters pushed under mats. The paint colours in his room were same as before. But the smells, the aromas seemed to be better; from an open window looking east and a dogwood tree on one side, laburnums in front and lawns further out. Rudi took to facing the window with the summer door open to be private, like it was a quiet moment in the barracks. He had the record player on with a 'swing' album, a cigarette on his lips, as he moved his feet over the floor to pose. He was like this in private: posing as old-timer in a chair, then forlorn lover on the bed, a neurotic veteran at the drink and he had all the props, genuine gear; hardwearing kit, den furniture and bottles of the right stuff – club whisky/ sherry /soda water, on the night table. It was a good scene, a great set, but no more players and no action.

Next month Rudi was at a local Pow Wow, on an Indian reserve at the river, where he met Yellowbird Folinsbee. She had been Joanne, at High School, because her mother was Scottish and her father a native Indian; when it mattered about her image as a teenager. Rudi sat on the stands with her to ask about the beaded costume she wore and her new name, but could not understand her quick answers. They watched the men's war-dance, infront of a dozen drums beaten hard and great feather costumes jumping in the late afternoon sun. It really was the same as days-of-old before the Europeans came, except for the glasses; two of them wore spectacles and one wore sunglasses. The beat was hard and fast as the feet stamped the dry grass arena; or younger men leapt around in clever patterns of agility and strength. The women cried out at the drums, into the microphones; cried out loud like baleful wolves in the den, except more angry, like creatures wanting attention and respect. Other tribes from far away as Alberta were present from Friday to Sunday when the grand procession closed with spirit prayers. Before that it was a comfortable Saturday afternoon, with a measured crowd giving equal attention to the stalls, the dances and authentic food. Rudi was chewing on a corn husk, the young woman too and talking, laughing at each other on a good middle-stand view.

When two veterans came to dance past, they looked and saw native men in Army khaki with band colours; you could see their service stripes and insignia among the tassels of leather, the pants each had a vertical stripe. They were dark and sinewy like old nut trees and veteran drinkers, smokers…

"Indians are good fighters too", she had to say.

"Yeah"?

"My father was a National Guardsman, for ten years".

"My father in Aircorps; one of the 'paleface' units"!

"Palefaces and White-eyes"!

"…and Yellow-bellies; you reckon Littlebird"?

"This corn's good; can you get some more please"?

"Indians were also good farmers", he had to say, stepping down from his seat to the firm ground beneath them.

"My grandfather a great hunter and a farmer".

"My grandpappy was a sailor, one of the invasion units".

"Invaders and colonists"!

"And settlers, good settlers" --

Rudi left her fixed in a seat as he wandered around the show ground for more sweet corn. She never looked round to him, staring ahead at her rights of ceremony, unseen to be moved unknown to be felt. There was much shyness in the air; the same pride for old warriors as young maidens, papoose and dog, blankets and feather bonnets. Rudi wanted a part of it, more than anything since he came home; because no one confronted him unfairly. There were no sudden questions, no demands; even if they did talk and joke together all afternoon-evening. There was a lot of conversation without upsetting him and no one wanted to be rude with his past. The pride here was good and it was intense, upright.

He brought back two hot-dogs instead of the corn and she took one without comment; they sat together again, silently this time, thinking of the food and each other in a private way. She was still lovely and fresh he realized, but didn't let on. Rudi was still a home-boy, who needed to touch base with girls he remembered shine out before he went away; still had their names on a Christmas list and one or two school photos. His own grad photo said, 'Rudi (Rudolph) Borah likes hunting without weapons, trekking without targets and baying at the moon – but settled for football this year and the swim team'. Yellowbird was Joanne in Nineteen-sixty-six with pony tail, fringe and tartan outfit; above: 'I need to find the world in a grain of sand, meet my friends on the horizon and bake new recipes for the family'. It was still like that in the album, a year behind Rudi, in Westside High School; he also knew her in the school band that year, when they got the horn parts wrong together time and again --

"Great to see you, Jo, really it was".

"You going"?

"Yeah, my father needs the truck tonight".

78

"Call me, okay". She moved over to clasp him by the arms, to lay her head on his shoulder and go quiet for the parting. He held her, then let go with a long hug; their arms and opposite shoulders taking the shared weight.

Before Rudi got to his vehicle, he took one more turn round the grounds, as if the last time for him or the Indians; he was unsure about something. Tonight he would be deep in his room again and on Sunday hidden in the garden corner like before. She seemed an interesting gal, he was thinking that night on his bed blankets; she related to the sounds of silence, same as him, was hip to the moment and right-on every time. It was not really a date for him, more like an encounter with a sister of the Promised Land, a face from the past. He never got much further with this as he drifted to sleep more easily than other nights. The bottles, the books, remained untouched and unwanted this time, because he was starting to come home at last. He didn't know how, but a home-coming was finally happening for him -

He saw his niece every Saturday, townspeople too, the neighbours and kids from school now at college; which was a lot of driving and walking even if not a lot of talking. He was covering a lot of ground and this was always important. The following Monday he went to see Mr. Wheldon again about career opportunities in the forestry service; yet he could not put Joanne out of his head. He stood before the telephone in the downstairs hallway on two evenings but left it at that each time. It appeared to be a big thing to call her, but he couldn't figure why, not exposing him to any danger. She would be at home, in the same town, yet that could be so remote from him. Of course this was the system in America; a pluralistic structure he could not decide about, if he should accept again after being away. The town manners were complicated, strict and tiresome, which is why he could not succeed in contacting her; manners on the telephone were even more difficult.

He was still getting fair treatment at home from his step-mother, no changes there. Away from the house the world was both inviting and hostile, or exciting and dull, challenging and cruel, which ever way he headed; over to the town center, the river bank, or meeting someone. He spent some evenings with his father, just talking together in the garden room. His father ate oranges and nuts as they skimmed topics together, happy to urge each other on. His step-mother usually had her time with Rudi in the morning, as she followed him through breakfast chores or drove him from the house by noon-time. Though he looked forward to his niece coming over to visit he never had anything to say to her mother. This was a lot of women to take into account for Rudi each week, to make him sleep soundly at night. But home is always a woman's camp; how they could make it comfortable or quickly uncomfortable if they wanted, when they got scared about the men and they got scared pretty quick about unlikely things.

One day Rudi was driving the loop road into town and remembered the library girls he waited for on the steps. Now he did not make an effort for them anymore and did not go inside the place either. He also left out the bus-stop and the river walk, because he had a woman to settle with. Rudi still walked out; but three times a week made sure he was at her place by eight-pm and Saturday they went out somewhere or called on friends. One Sunday he went to the store with her father and they joked out loud together at the cashier lady. Joanne always fitted him in and took no heed of the state in which he arrived. She did not go to his house, was shy to visit; but stopped-by once from her evening job at a local diner and was free-an-easy with his step-mother on the telephone.

Rudi was often thinking how they might be more intimate, when he came to relax in his room at home. By the time they met-up Joanne did all the talking about it and he pretended to be surprised and coy. The next week he was under her bed covers, quiet and lazy, or pushing her into the rear of the vehicles they used. It was harmless fun, cozy and warm. She rebuked him all the time, but not enough to spoil it, because he was confused and fragile about her. But she did upset him with the group of friends they saw; how she greeted these other men with embarrassing gusto and Rudi was left in the kitchen fixing drinks, washing things, or listening to someone unhappy. Seems the more happy he became the more vulnerable; he already knew that to be happy was because you had been unhappy, or were about to be. Before all this, he was not unhappy just lonely, which is quite different. In fact, to be lonely was to become strong; men had to be lonely and not show it. To be unhappy made Rudi angry because it meant he missed something, he'd made a mistake with something or someone. Women were unhappy a lot, but they could share it around so easily. Rudi would also make Joanne unhappy soon because it was over three months he saw her; which put a lot of pressure upon him. He had to joke a lot, have lots of places to go and things for them to do; a full responsibility for him.

Eventually, Rudi got a job acceptable to him and took a loan to buy his own vehicle. It was up-state with a timber company at a water-shed area and friends said they were supportive. Joanne bought him dinner at the Trout Farm place; he picked the wine and promised to eat slow. Not everyone was happy the same way; how his step-mother wanted him to stay in his room and avoid rent payments. But the work-site was a long journey at morning, if he stayed out the night before. She was very talkative about it and fussed over the food more, followed him about the house as he gathered up some of his things to take away, usually when his father was absent. His father wanted this job badly for Rudi and all that went with it: the truck, the girl, work and paychecks. However Rudi did turn to his step-mother one day and promised to try college the next year.

He wanted to do more things, please more people and not be secretive about it; until he shot himself one afternoon in the garden, in the small yard beside a tool shed. His hunting rifle put a slug into the side of his chest; which meant he went straight to the infirmary that same hour. There was enough blood on the lawn and some logs nearby, to cause serious concern, but he was conscious when carried away.

"I'm sorry, I'm sorry", he kept saying to anyone. He could forget about working and moving now, or even driving his truck. He couldn't go with his girl either, or scout the river paths. His father said he did not know what he meant by 'sorry'; definitely did not understand. Was he sorry for shooting himself like that, trying to hurt himself maybe, or sorry for the trouble he made. His step-mother insisted it was unexpected when she saw some hand-tools and cloths on the garden table and remembered how he never would clean a gun in the house or in his room. It had to be an accident she told his father and the police when they arrived. No one could ask Rudi, as he lay in the care unit; because he kept slipping in-an-out of consciousness that first week, in front of vigilant visitors who sat close by the clever medical machines.

"Oh Rudi, we hardly knew you; but we're still here" Joanne said to him as she waited at the bedside and tried to figure when she should leave for home, when to return next day. There wasn't much to see, the same scene each time; but he was there, definitely there in the bed wanting to tell her what happened; when he took hold of a familiar object in the garden on an ordinary day, to attend routine mechanical service needed. "Oh Rudi, come back to us", she repeated in front of his parents and again when the doctor came by with no definite answers for them.

CHAPTER EIGHT

A young Indian boy came into the first-aid station on a very hot day. He had been fishing, straight after breakfast, on his own. But he got tired by the afternoon and had an accident, which required help. The fish hook had gone into his hand and would not come out.

The nurse was from town, but happy to attend boys in their summer camp; her job until September when the schools would start again. Mostly she saw boys with sunburn or cuts from swimming among the rocks. But this time it was a lad about eleven years old, who loved fishing in the creek, like the rest of his tribe would.

He held out his left hand and looked directly into her face to seek some kindness and care. His open palm showed a hook embedded in the flesh across from the thumb and going very still she examined the injury; asking her questions about the fishing and how to work his line. He tried to talk and answer normally, to distract himself from the pain. It was a small hook used to catch fishlets, sprats and such like, at the water's edge; not really for bigger fish. But the barb was well into the heel of his hand and she could not pull it out. The nurse finally explained to the boy how they would push it through and out the other side – the only way she knew. He began to wince and tense as she began pushing and started to cry-out when seeing the barb go further into his hand. By the time it appeared to be coming out, the boy was staring at the floor-boards beneath him and grabbing his wrist with the other hand, trying not to give-in or cry out again --

"Almost there, almost out" she kept saying, "just a bit more". But he was not listening anymore, only holding on tight and glaring at the floor between them. He was a tough little Indian boy, but the hook was made of steel and the barb was cruel.

WORK MATES

Young men should work in construction, or a farm; some place where they get dirty and measure up to older men, tougher men. This is because in any man's life, hard work and dirty war is never far away. Working a big construction site in the far north of the country, is not new, but still a good idea --

"Borah, where is he; Rudi Borah"? A heavy set engineer scraped over the safety-sill to find a young man with a drill team, in a hole, on the dam site.

"Here, over here", giving notice to the supervisor who originally hired him and in late season.

"Treat these men right Rudi? You ain't on top here, okay! Do your job for me and fall in with these men; get that"?

"Yes sir, Mister Warder" and two generations walked off together to the shack where Rudi rushed up some coffee for his boss and stood straight infront moving a hard-hat up from his face.

"You got these reports licked Rudi, good on yuh! No problem there. Let me show you the projection for this task. See the drill patterns; we need a grout pattern to seal-off this rock -- can you do that for us? See if we can't keep you anyway"!

Rudi saw his job taken away, replaced and moved, approved and tested, between two or three gulps of coffee; but didn't show anything except to shift weight over his stance and go quiet. It was about personalities up on the Peace River; conservative men shaking hands together on a number of issues: work ethics, dress codes, sexual preferences and drink habits. The politics of construction was self-evident and based on good grounds; because it could be dangerous with big payouts.

"Get yourself some new boots, toe-capped. And another thing; what's the mess on your face? First thing up top, son, I buy you a razor-blade"! Mr. Warder waved his lower arms about like flagging someone and puffed at his shortened cigar-butt; downed his mug onto the bench and headed away with some force. Rudi was a youthful strength needing to be re-active, not pro-active, needing to be compliant and resilient. He learned all this in rugby football, at his school back home, where you passed the ball back to move forward. His father sent Rudi to his own school, so he could go on to be something. Rudi rebelled against any career; but was in accord with his grandfather, an early settler in the West. It was blood to the fore and Rudi set to quit this site at sometime and travel back with a good grubstake.

His job was all-found up on the Yukon border; a hydro project with near two thousand seasonal work-force housed in traditional northern territory bunk-houses. Rudi related like it was military service; like a summer field exercise with Mr. Warder as colonel of the brigade and himself a junior rank at the work-face down in the power house chambers, to be grouted and sealed for the oncoming water flow next year. You could see he was proud of his position in the working of things; sure of his worth in physical endeavours and enjoying relocation to a land of men without women. It was also relocation to a terrain without confines, without spoilage and excessive amounts of sky/air. His room was only a place to sleep, not an abode, as Rudi went to other bunk-houses to read or play guitar. He went to drink beer on Saturday and off to swim anytime as it was still August; nearby was a swimming hole, where local Indians cooled off and played in clean water. Rudi stuck to masses of lengths, with several strokes, like he learned in High School. They simply enjoyed each other in another idle summer; while he needed to unwind and practise a solitary exercise. The boys were pushing each other into the deep end for the fun of it; the older pair simply enjoyed wading clean blue water. Rudi trawled up-an-down one side, with alternate swim strokes, until his respiration picked up strongly. He was working hard, but not competing with Indians at traditional lazy play. He tried to see how they differed from native Indians, closer to his home; how they were short and dark, less proud.

They were still at play, when Rudi tugged on his pants and headed to camp; they not noticing/minding him cross their patch of territory to leave for the day. He got up to the shack serving as bull-kitchen for the camp, to select cut sandwiches from the container tins and went to put them with the brown beers he had under his bunk -- because it was coming to Saturday night. But two young men were waiting for him, sitting on his bed -- "We have to leave camp Rudi"!

"What's up"?

"The Mounties were in town to get fire-fighters. A fire broke out on Portage Mountain and they cleared out the bar. We took your beers; okay"?

"Where are they"?

"They're coming up here; so let's go"! The three young men went out behind the bunkhouse, to find to a hollow in the brush; seeing Garth and Jason already there, lounging on stick piles eating and smoking.

"Where you been" said Garth?

"To get Rudi and his liquor".

"Don't forget the grub, I got -- but that's mine, you damn Canucks"!

"Up yours, you redneck jug-head"!

"Stupid Limey, this is your fault, got a limey name stamped all over it"!

"Yeah, how"?

"Mischievous liability, individual negligence -- A DAMN STUPID SMOKER"!

The two men jumped at each other like angry bears and wrestled across the dry undergrowth, far as they could go, in a hot evening on the mountain side. When tired and overheated they fell apart thirsty and hungry, while Garth openly put his cigarette pack away. Then they whined-on about the resultant liquor shortage; with five young men were hiding out all night and too close together for comfort.

"Maybe the fire-service ain't so bad".

"They get a dollar an-hour and grub".

"Wieners and beans -- and a blanket. Don't forget the blanket roll".

"Garth was at a fire, last season, right? Tell us about it Englishman"!

"Yeah we all got blankets and don't forget the shovel, we also got a shovel. I ended up cooking wieners-an-beans every day; because the cooks kept running away and after two weeks I ran away"!

"After you volunteered to serve, asshole! When you went for a closer look and got nabbed for it. Ha-ha"!

"A real adventure and informing my curiosity about Canada".

"Stupid damn Limey and his warm beer".

"No chance to wash or get out of smoky gear; just flung stuff away when I returned to my job".

"Almost lost your job"!

"No, my credit to brave the fire and try new things -- Mister Warder said he admired reckless bravado, since he left the Army corps".

"... Since he grew old"!

"... Is why he came up to Canada"!

Well past dusk they laughed at each other and with each other; about their work, about Mr. Warder and summer fires. By eleven-pm new appetites forced them to risk a visit to the bull-kitchen for more choice sandwiches. Garth started passing his cigarettes round as they approached the compound and Rudi took a look for police wagons, or worrying signs of capture. Mike was still at the card table, as ever; with a poker hand across from a big pile of pay-checks with dollar bills in between.

"Been here long, Mike"?

"All night" he responded with Russian accent and stone face, "why"?

"No police raid tonight? No Mounties here"!

"No; but I heard about Portage Mountain and the bar in town emptied to help out. I'm too old; they want you boys. Better return to your cradle in the bush for a few days. Young blood is under-supply but underpaid. I need to cover my bets, so no chance to see myself digging fire breaks with the unlucky and the unwashed"!

"See yuh. I'm tired and in no need of the same company tonight".

The Mounties had not arrived at camp; but no one was sure for the next week. Stories were big of the August fires round the watershed timber; tinder-dry and ready to light-up, with a ready supply of useful men at hand.

Rudi read for a while, then slept well after tired of thinking over fire-duty concerns. The next three nights no police came, but men were scarce and quiet about losing their paying job to go with the forest service; a serious loss in pay slips and camp comforts. Rudi knew he could lose his job and would be easily replaced in the crew - - though he never served at a fire before, something in him wanted to try, if only for his own rough qualifications. He loved the woods as a boy when his father took the guns out for unsuspecting game on the mountain-side. But Rudi realized his father never intended to shoot anything, the way they slogged off into a wet dawn to hop from one false trail to another; not to kill any animal -- just carrying and nursing two rifles with satchels all day up-an-down the gullies -- knowing his father was a veterinarian. He could have also been a teacher the way real lessons were disguised and extended: like escaping home suburbs and women's kitchens; to refind first territory and remaking home in the forests with the speechless creatures still residing there. Rudi never went out hunting with boys from camp, because there were no hidden mercies from these types; when they raced off in fortified pick-ups after over-dosing on early caffeine.

All week ahead Rudi was at the same penstock shaft with Mike from the concrete section. He was at the drill set-up and counting rod pieces to check entry depth; carrying cement bags to the grout mixer and sharing the labour involved. Mike was on the re-bar steel and checking the quality for making good concrete surfaces with a new grade mix. He was up and down the intake wall and fell off coming down, hitting the stony ground hard, but tore his hand on the steel up the wall; near lost a finger and came over to Rudi's shack to look-see.

"It needs the Doc, Mike".

"Where is he today -- at camp"?

"No, at the top compound, back of the secretary's office".

"Get me up there, will yuh Rudi. Don't let me lose my card-playing finger. You can get a company vehicle to ride -- yeah"!

"Okay, follow me; it's not your foot that's hurt".

Rudi drove them up to office shacks on the transmission site and led Mike to an examination table.

"Get that stuff off his hand so I can see", said the doctor. "What we got here? Looks like no hunting for you awhile".

"What'd'you mean"?

"This trigger finger is fractured good and surrounding ligaments torn bad".

"I play cards -- no hunting -- or I make the women happy".

"And with one hand for a while, maybe".

"Good enough for me".

"-- but not good enough for two men in the diversion tunnels"!

"What"?

"-- like, they won't need hands again".

"How d'you mean"?

"-- must be dead by now. An explosion, this morning down at the river and two of the drill team took the full blast. They're already into town at the infirmary -- I never saw to it up here".

Rudi and Mike went quiet and polite to allow more come out about the lower project site, not heeded much because almost complete and sub-contracted.

"Seems the safety officer..."

"A real asshole, if you ask me".

"... seems he called the play last year, gave a warning. Anyway, there always was gas and these two were isolated and careless; they got a belly-full of rock shot no hard-hat could stop. I went to the scene but handed straight over to the ambulance when I saw limp bodies with a lot more blood than dust on their gear; not even a whisper or groan from their faces. Yeah, too late for me. Maybe the relatives will get up there tonight; more help than me now".

"Is work stopped at the tunnels now, Doc"?

"No, they got another crew back in there today".

"The safety officer is also production officer by proxy"!

"They got to get the rock cleared Mike", said Rudi as he gathered-in to head off.

"And it won't be a memorial site" said the doctor.

"I gotta leave and get back to my crew. Maybe they also want to know about the accident". Rudi went through the offices to hear more about the explosion and two unlucky 'Joes'; innocent working stiffs with likely widows and families down in the city; blood on the job, tears at home, a mess in production. The office ladies were also concerned, but continued working at typewriters and paper anyway. Rudi got out the door into the vehicle, to be alone with his thoughts on scenes at the tunnel. He thought how they must have been unlucky with gas leaks; how he was lucky with risks taken every week down intake tunnels attending big turbine engines, or the way he drove vehicles close to the edge of the dam fill. God seemed to be cruel with the luck that goes around and who dies because of it.

He could see in the rear-view mirror his beard gaining recognition, definition, way beyond the limits for Mr. Warder. He rubbed his fingers over the bristle while the engine idled. Maybe the dead miners never tried a beard. They wanted to try but never did; now they couldn't and would always be remembered as clean shaven. Rudi wanted to see how it would grow, what it could look like, how it might change him. It was still easy for him to slip into gear and drive off to camp without Mike and guess if it was steak and potatoes for dinner, or beans and pork. Two men died, Mike almost lost a finger, but he hadn't lost his appetite. He drove the same way from the office compound up to the spillway road as a lazy detour; then slowed down for a bird's-eye view of the whole project. Hot sun intensified the location at four-pm; top of the day with maximum number of men at work mid-week and no brakes anywhere. The valley had once curved at this point, but was re-made into a corner between two heights either side of the diversion tunnel. The Peace River was an endless shape of royal blue with a blue-wash sky, bordered by tree lines, arranging the natural elements into recognition of a memorable landscape -- rebutted by the project workings before him when colours and shapes had been torn-up to reveal dusty material heaps, ragged lines of breaking structures and the flimsy shapes of frame dwellings. No father this time; Rudi had no father figure with him as he contemplated the territory he saw from height of day; on his own with a new generation of rough-necks. The farm veterinarian would never want to come out here, not even for Rudi and Rudi wouldn't want that. It often takes a long journey to break away from home.

By this time his feet were up on the dashboard and he desired to light-up a smoke. He searched his kit for a cigarette and focused inside the cab; to see a scratched enamel capsule as both transport and protection from the unthinking forces around him. At end of smoking he went down on the clutch and moved-off to track back to the intake tunnels again. It was still hot with a hard glare on the windscreen and dust clouding up at every action of vehicles on the ground. Heat and dust all over a Yukon August, over any honest endeavour; no escaping this mantle of northern summer because it was still God's country and God was a man.

When he got to the grout shack he saw Mr. Warder at the bench with coffee mug and cigar; more blue-prints and talk over the table to a foreman --

"Say Rudi, we got a new plan to follow. How say you"?

"Can I take a look"?

"Sure -- where yuh come from just now? I wanna get back up top before shift change".

"The Doc's office; we had an accident, injury today".

"Yeah, we heard something"... to set awkwardness between the men as tragedy was inferred so quickly and so evenly.

"I mean Mike Horvath; near lost a finger on the re-bar steel", which got even less attention from the project manager. He tugged at his belt then his cigar with the same hand, as he returned to familiar business upon the prints -- drill schedules, projected times and measures. Rudi looked over to Mr. Warder as they held steady over calculations; to see a plain faced man with lots of ruddy skin, grey eyes, dark eyebrows and army-style haircut. His hard-hat left a crease mark across his head and the summer sun had burned behind his ears and across his neck. There were no unnecessary movements; there was strength of purpose, a quiet lifestyle and need to be the boss. His khaki outfit was really like a uniform without the spit-an-polish; no polish up here, but small signs of rank upon the man. His voice was the first sign; he always got to be heard. He liked to see everything and everyone, because he was the man on top.

"I know about Mike. He's a Ruskie, a White Ruskie from China; escaped to Canada after the Reds took over. He's walking history, a talking education after the card games. Me and Ivan here were on the other side of the war, the European theatre, enjoying a continental campaign".

Rudi blanched at the new info he just heard, about hard-ass Mr. Warder and the foreman close by. He waited for more as he stepped nearer to the bench; waited for more talk or engineer's directives.

"... I went to Italy first".

The foreman nodded at points made, to comply.

"...Italy, then France, where I got my first vines. Yuh see I'm a wine-maker now -- after hiding in a vineyard near Monza for several days – impressionable, I guess".

"I became a smoke-a-holic" added the foreman, "brought home a baggage load of vices"!

"You not even born then -- well just about" and Rudi enjoyed some scant acknowledgment. Wanting to hear more he bowed over the plans and figures, but disturbed the men with rank and position at the bench, as they swapped service details a few minutes more.

"Gotta get up top". Mr. Warder suddenly swept memories aside and laughed at the foreman; combed his hair with fat fingers, rolled a blue-print under his arm and went out to the grout header attached to a drill hole; followed by Rudi taking his cue to go alongside.

"Follow these hook-ups; we gotta account for gallons of mix each shift and each intake. Leave the section papers till end and watch these connections".

"Okay, fine. I already do".

"I like Mike and a game of cards, myself, Texas rules. But better not miss any work shifts, if he shows at the poker tables tonight. See yuh" -- stomping ahead to a pickup truck with short-arm wave over his shoulder and hard grasp of the chrome door handle. Rudi watched him exit in good robust style because this was his show, he the main player with all the juice.

When Rudi got back to the grout shack the foreman looked at him as if they were now related, since not everyone heard their war stories. He offered Rudi a cigarette before they started climbing down the ladders. Rudi was shy about smoking and nervous of the steps, when he had to talk and find his way down three hundred feet of eighty-percent incline, from the intake to the powerhouse. Many steps were missing in the thirty minute descent and parts of the hoop-round safety cage were also missing. The first time Rudi went down, a drill team were arguing and sending up machine sparks to scare the new crewman at entrance to the hole. He began walking the incline then turned round to go on all-fours, descending the tunnel the same way water would next year. It was fifteen feet across and level at the intake for twenty feet, before sloping down to the incline where water would fall hundreds of feet to the powerhouse below; the powerhouse cut into solid rock beneath a mantle of the fillway. At the very bottom a cast-iron turbine wheel sat on a bolted platform, to catch the falling torrents and turn the big iron blades round-an-round. Rudi counted ten turbines in the powerhouse, to take water from the same number of tunnels. A lot of crews centered their work at this site; it had to be ready first if the dam was to work. It was a big ship-size chamber, with derricks and gantries constantly traversing the long open space –

Mike Horvath walked with bow legs like a real westerner, but he hailed from the East, the Far East. He wore his hard-hat to cover a bald patch because he liked women and wanted them to like him, not just for his paycheck or generosity with liquor. He often took a couple of cases of brew to the reserve on a warm night and stayed a few days. But he liked Russian women once and Chinese women in Peking. He told Rudi about them and showed his pictures -- the water-colours which he painted all over the site. They were good pictures of men at work and different scenes of the project in winter, then summer -- but nothing in style or art, for artists. Mike was now old -- tall and grey round the ears, but slim with a bright eye. In fact, he had more in common with young people, because they admired him; leaving the past to others and happy in the moment.

Rudi went to Mike's bunkhouse to find him entertaining young surveyors with vodka. Surveyors were meant to be first into unknown territory and cool with it. Mike took his vodka like a drought was coming and the survey boys sipped their portions in turn. They were very young, tall, lean and enjoying an unknown liquor. Mike was about to head off to the reserve and the boys were going into town; departing of ways more than a generation parting. Rudi took his drink and named the swimming hole as destination; swim and sun, like winter was coming early that year. But they all started off together in a company wagon and Mike wanted to join Rudi for some coffee at the main store in town, before they also parted ways.

"Just going to the 'john' before I sit".

"Okay Mike".

"Yes, wadda you boys want" said the waitress?

"Two coffees".

"Any pie"?

"What"?

"We got apple pie or pumpkin, blueberry, boysenberry, peach, cherry or"--

"Any pecan"?

"No. How about cheesecake; strawberry or --"?

"Okay, any kinda cheesecake. Bring over a piece each, please".

"With or without cream"?

"No cream, give us two forks instead. Thanks".

She was a local native, about nineteen years old and well used to men and what they did in the north; but nervous just the same. Her eyes moved back-an-forth a lot, anxiously, yet her voice was flat and even. She went easily between the kitchen and counter top; wiping and clearing all the while she answered Rudi. Her hair was medium under a white ribbon head-band; her colour dusky and durable. Not a pretty Indian maiden, but sturdy and useful -- the kind western men took over when first coming into this area and now lots of half-breeds in northern territories. This girl was full-blood from a local tribe, at home in the café; but shy of customers as if she had something to lose in the bigger world, something to lose from any contact outside her village. Mike sat down and talked to her straight-off. Not really the way Rudi was, often more quiet than anyone; how he preferred sit and watch. But they were each at cross-purposes again; for the girl was at work and they off-work with time and money to spend.

CHAPTER NINE

The young man took a book off the shelf, then another, before he found a good choice to read. It was a sea-adventure and he started at the middle pages, like he often did when it was a new find. Suddenly an older man appeared in the same aisle. It was the owner of the drug store, who usually made-up prescriptions or took money at the cash register. But today he walked between the rows of goods and stood right infront of the young man reading –

"Enjoying the book" he said "is it really good"?

"Well, yeah" --

"So can I get a chair or something, make you more comfortable, sound alright"!? Of course he had been seen reading before, in this store, quietly perusing the paper-back section. The owner was trying to be sarcastic, to make the other man feel awkward and embarrassed, making a bit of public display.

But the younger man lived in central California before, where he often browsed in a store like this. No one would pay any attention if he did not buy a book. Lots of people he saw read the same way: trying different topics, enjoying new print, the text layout and coloured covers; to forget about more pressing concerns of the day...

Nothing more to say now, the young man went off in the direction of a local café he knew, because he also liked walking out and eating.

A SPRING BREAK

Rudi Borah was from working stock, which meant a lot of time fully occupied with dirty jobs, honest labor for his father and paid work too. But he was also a dreamer, a restless lad who bayed at the moon and equated distance travelled the same as lessons learned and books read, colleges attended. His father had been the same and his mother a vexed woman who wished for a daughter as constant company, a full compliment in her house. This month in Spring, Rudi arranged two weeks off his employment, to utilize the open highways and test his vehicle repairs, see how far it would go without more of his attention.

His small town was circled by mountains and Rudi could not take his eyes off them. They were not peaks, but large round hills completely covered in trees; like they had been painted over by God himself. These mountains were very imposing, looming large in the landscape; yet they often looked close enough to touch. Rudi sometimes felt he could reach out and grasp the green foliage, or poke his finger into a mint blue stream to let its coolness wash the soreness off his palms. Every evening Rudi went into the streets to find his new friends, before the dark came. He turned each way to see hills in the east and one to the south; noticed how at dusk they appeared darker than before and looked like they were moving closer towards him. At dusk colours faded and the big shapes before him became warm shades of sepia, till they were only a silhouette on the horizon, a feint line glowing round him as the sun deserted them once more.

One day Rudi finally fixed his truck and wanted to drive out; leaving this small town and sing along with his radio as the road stretched infront, reaching into the same scenes he saw every day from home. For two hours Rudi sat at his wheel and stared ahead at the cafe-stops passing, the fences, cabins and road signs. There was no one to talk with but nothing to say about the power of ancient rock, the sweetness of streams rushing under bridges he crossed, a massing of forest scents. Rudi found a camp-site at end of day and parked his vehicle to eat some travel food. He sighted trail signs marked to show the lake views ahead; a long shape of silvered water sparkled under last light and threaded a broken line behind the tree cover. He was driving the night before too, not like he wanted; but making good distance before sleeping, because it was still further to travel the next day. Since he got a new vehicle, there were lots of places to go; news leaked out and he was in demand, one way or another. When not mobile, no one called he remembered, they forgot about him.

It was a long dull drive and raining out, to make it more dull; Rudi could not see anything except the road ahead and the lights behind. Music blared out from the dash and he tried humming along, slapping his thigh to the beat of CW favourites -- thinking about what transpired the night before, another longing phone call from a plaintive gal. But the traffic was enough to keep Rudi's mind on the road and a cop cruiser pulled infront of him to get all his attention for a while; making Rudi squirm in his seat as if already guilty of something unspeakable, unforgettable. The cop vehicle was a two-tone coup with lamps and decals like out of a toy-box; but the car was real alright and the cops a real nuisance sometimes, like bugs in the sun or flies in the house. It was a bad omen at such time of night, worrying and perturbing, because Rudi was tired and not ready for trouble. The CD player went onto side two and reminded him how the cab of a vehicle can be comforting and secure, while it moved; like a time capsule going towards the future, along with other vehicles; trying to catch-up on missed items and past disappointments. Moving was always good and driving the state highway in a Ford roadster was American as apple pie.

He was headed to another small town on the coast and when he crested the last hill he could taste salty air from the sea and gulls were calling out in familiar chorus. There were big heritage houses sited on the cliffs looking serious and majestic, facing the ocean and town centre at the same time, nestled upon a small river site going into the harbour. There was lots of colour with various stores and the bunting; shrubs and flower beds bordered the sidewalks and people seemed happy the way they strolled across the street with no particular place to go. 'Difficult to get yuh headup-your-arse in a place like this', he thought. Two cops met at a corner, licking at ice-cream cones, with their caps pushed up high. It was like this all over San Lorenzo, with open calmness and slow reactions; warm and bright too. 'A good place, a nice town, for a young lady to reside', when he thought more about it. He came into town specially to see her again, after years away up in Canada.

"You still got your own teeth" she would ask? "Are they for real"?

"I was going to ask you, about being blonde, if you still coloured your hair" he answered.

After Rudi got to the house and started to feel comfortable he had to leave and find somewhere else to sleep, because he could not stay. Her father would find him in the morning and be angry, even if he slept alone on the floor – because she was only sixteen. Her father loved her more than the other sister, was more protective. So before darkness came, she took him and his gear up the road, alongside some grassy fields and Rudi got out. He borrowed her down sleeping bag and kissed her cheek, like he thought was right, then set off to find a place to lie down.

It was a bright starry night as he lay face-up to the sky, with his head on rolled-up pants and gear at his feet; he was alright, was okay. He came to find the girl, to see her again after some fretful phone calls and a letter – but no matter, he enjoyed this camping out. He was alone and free and men can be happy like that; lots of men lived the same way for a long time. The crescent-shaped moon came out as beloved icon and glided infront of the stars, to watch over the honorable suitor without lodging. A deep-blue sky bent over him from one horizon to the other; birds roosted in trees above and people in town slept behind locked doors. He awoke next day to first light and sounds of traffic on the road nearby – two crows were perched above him, fluttering together, when he started to move. Rudi had no thought to seek the girl today, not now; he needed sustenance and some time to himself. His vehicle was parked out of sight and finding it safe he drove off to locate a low-cost diner he already knew about --

The screen door went to slam shut as Rudi stepped back about twenty or more years into an old style cafe, that sported neon at the front and formica table-tops inside. He was self-conscious at once knowing how everyone was watching, looking at the stranger choose a seat and listen to the way he talked, what he said – "Coffee, please and some eggs, toast" as he slid behind a table "scrambled, with hashed potatoes; thanks", he said

The cafe lady offered all kinds of extras as Rudi fiddled with the menu card and shuffled on his stool, realizing he still the main object of attention. But it was a small cafe, a small town and Rudi had something else to think about. He glanced out the window to help think of a route to follow, to find his friends in new places and continued like this while he waited. Occasionally he turned his head and looked round to the other customers, just as they looked down into their plates. It seemed polite to look at different patrons and think of them for a moment and he did the same with the waitress. But looking round the establishment was to see a dingy space with a bored waitress and lazy people; nothing pleasant. Looking outside was better and he aimed to get moving soon as he finished.

"Where you from, not round here, that's for sure" – she was directly infront of him looking for an answer, curious and distrustful. "More coffee – yeah"?

"No, water with lemon, please" – this was confusing for her, not what she expected.

And it was dark in the cafe, dark enough for lights-on everywhere, hanging listlessly above the tables. They gave off a yellow light, like the cafe was sick, the patrons or the food. Food smells from days before lingered in the air, cleaning agents and grease fought each other too long; stale odours and tired fixtures predominated. It was also a bit dusty; but didn't seem to matter and people were not about to move off in a hurry. Trees outside the window bordered a picture view up the road, out of town away from the cafe place; where Rudi just came from and where he headed to. This was only a 'pit stop', he reminded himself.

"Hey slow down kid, you're too hard on people and yourself" – she was back infront of Rudi wielding a big glass coffee flask, dark brown and hot, hanging on her worn fingers like she considered throwing it. He might have expected this because she read his mind, which was not difficult; he was never secretive, even when quiet and shy. For a bit of distraction he tried an old ploy, a parlour game he learned from home. He tried to figure who was married in the cafe, who out-of-work, a farmer or... while he ate and cleaned his plate, paid his bill and made last comments to the lady. There was a married couple at coffee, sitting opposite each other unsmiling; he correctly spotted two farmers by their hands and boots and saw a chain-smoker loafing in the corner. But was Rudi only passing through, like he thought, or was life passing him by? Suddenly, it seemed as if things were turned inside-out, like two dimensions of his life had intersected; how the cafe people were now on the inside of everything and himself the small boy again, shut out and unhappy.

Up the roadway forked in two directions and one way was unknown to him as befitted his mood, contemplative and self-conscious. He drove up to a dead-end, which opened into parking and a chance to take his quest a bit further. 'Our Lady of Victories' the sign said, 'visitors welcome' and it seemed a good opportunity to hear what another voice had to say from a different point of view. Rudi went into the church and found an old priest presiding, as an oracle, waiting to be heard. He sat at the front to one side and enjoyed the hymns remembered from childhood. He escaped the big wide world for a while and regressed to a boy again, when Sunday was open and free, away from school and parents. Rudi sat still with the prayers to feel a lot of guilt and shame coming over him, when he read his own secret fears and doubts in the service sheets, for everyone to know. Bible lessons were direct and on-target about distractions in the wicked world, from very old texts; yet at the same time sentences were fresh and strong, impossible to be ignored --

Back outside again, the sun was shining onto some boats moored infront of a seawall, he noticed. They were sailboats mostly with their white hulls catching the reflected light and they danced on the water, swelling for the morning tide change. He walked straight off in that direction, to realize how he was attracted like birds to the berries, like young men to the ladies. 'That's why boats are female' he mused, 'specially sailboats, regarded as beautiful women when their sails unfurl; unpredictable and winsome, compelling and capricious'. He kept walking along the harbor wall, to check what he thought over, then circled back to the church yard. It was the biggest green patch in town, with flower beds and landscaping; an old style graveyard, not common now when people used cremation for their loved ones. Rudi took a turn round the lawns on the sunny afternoon, when he had no special place to go and no loved ones to think about. There was a gardener tending the grass and edges, who seemed to jump when he approached –

"Never heard you come in" said the man, "didn't notice your truck"!

"I left it behind" Rudi replied "and walked in here" realizing the man was spooked a little; the way he talked fast and speeded-up his work, as if caught-out by the boss or someone threatening.

Rudi stood before a newly dug hole, covered with wooden boards to stop anyone falling in and the dirt heaped at one side, ready to be shovelled back. 'It must be hard to bury family', he glancing at the name plates; 'specially a child, put into a small box and see it buried, then to walk away. Maybe a coffin will arrive tomorrow, for this place, along with the burial party'. The next space over was also a fresh site; the coffin already in the ground and dirt shoved into the hole to leave a bare track on top, as if someone had stolen the grass sod. Cut flowers lay all over the place with paper notes attached; a very colorful scene, a pretty site, for such a sad occasion.

But time for reflection was over, he needed get back onto the road; to make some distance between the girl and himself, between unsettling feelings and his forward motion. He went north for the Bay area, but managed to ride the coast road; to accentuate the journey and slow-down the intake of impressions. Rudi drove through the middle of day, looking out left at the Pacific Rim everyone was talking about, to see successive waves of white foam breaking onto the beach. Though there was no one about to follow the water-line today; only Rudi was available to attend the enormity of this scene -- how the sea rolled into the coast like this for a million years, how seabirds always scoured the shore for food and how sand-grass constantly fought the wind to reclaim the land. These were big conflicts ensuing, long standing conflicts of shore-life over sea-life, of land over water and life over the void. After an hour or so like this, Rudi steered off the road into a vacant lot and turned round to face the ocean directly. He had a beverage flask on the rear seat; so got off the front seat to lean-up against a warm radiator with milky coffee, enjoying a whole view – a million grains of sand beneath every wave, everlasting winds from the west rushing across foamy crests and the strength of evolution within a deep ocean. All this wonder and mystery just for him, as true sentinel of his time, a solitary traveler and lonesome heart.

Rudi finally lay across the back seat, to sleep, in his big chevie cruiser. It was late in San Francisco and he was tired, too tired to drive home; so he reached for the blankets which stayed on the rear seats and got his head down. His vehicle was parked in a back alley in North Beach, which should have been private and safe for one night. He had visited the famed bookstore, Ferlinghetti's City Lights, till closing at midnight, searching for who-knows-what; suitably tired, very full, after a day out in the city. In the rear was an old style bench seat, to allow him stretch out under a blue pattern woolen, with his rolled pants on the armrest as pillow and windows open a fraction for air. He ran the engine earlier, to get some heat going inside; then lay back to take his chances with the police, local busybodies, or anything else going bump in the night. He slept immediately, nestled comfortably under the edge of his quilt, with only toes sticking out from the cover. Rudi did not dream, but neither did he worry anymore about his vehicle up an unknown alley. He was set to get the rest he deserved, as young man upon his travels from the coast, to see old friends and new sights in the city.

But a few hours into his vigil he awoke, hearing another car approaching from behind; concerned who it might be or what trouble it may bring. He was apprehensive about the unknown vehicle, the

104

noise and people involved; because it was late and he alone, vulnerable. It seemed the other car was approaching slowly, trying to go past, get between him and the far-side wall. He could feel the nearness of the second vehicle, how it was gingerly approaching the gap and attempting the passage. Rudi was always aware how his own car was big with broad beam, not leaving much space in the alley; the other driver could never pass freely, folly for him to try. But the vehicle kept coming and began to negotiate the opening. Rudi was alarmed and convinced it would scrape the fenders and do damage. He could bear it no longer and wanted to see what happened, so rose from his slumber to look out the side window. Sure enough, the car was passing, with two men in the front seats peering out to navigate. One of them, the driver on this side, saw Rudy and the blanket cover. He was young enough to be alert at such an hour and read a lot into the situation; enjoying his own take on what he saw, producing some salty humour.

"Hey pal, we see you and way to go, buddy"! He cried out and jerked his arm up to simulate carnal action; to make his joke clear, to signal Rudi and score points. They scraped clear and kept going, to leave Rudi behind with his auto comforts; the pants at his head, shoes together at the front − he was empty of baggage, far from home and nowhere near any female.

A few hours later, he forgot about this comical episode and awoke early before his auto attracted more unfavorable attention. Rudi was hungry again and had no hesitation to eat by then; the best possible reason to wake up and depart away. This time he went north across the harbour bridge to favour a plain menu and low prices, good food and full satisfaction. It was the remnants of an Indian reserve on the edge of Sonoma County, up to the hills on a forgotten trail. The Indian kids were at a breakfast café; a smorgasbord buffet and they loaded plates with cream pie and cake, instead of bacon and eggs. All across the table was jam jelly and blobs of white cream, stir sticks and spoons. The girl had chocolate cake and cream, along with orange juice and she was over-weight for a girl-child, with loaded cheeks and swollen arms; heavy to move in her soft seat. The parents were nearby, close enough to speak and listen, but blind to their indulgences; not seeing the mess or the stupidity. Rudi was right across from them with his brown toast and coffee, a tidy portion and clean space. He had a letter out across the table to compose a few thoughtful lines to his father, long overdue, in another state further east. Rudi wanted adventures away from home, he told his father; to ride over every mountain, to count the trees upon the slopes and learn how lakes sat at the bottom of everything, green and deep, cold and still. But he also saw a lot of other things close-up, like ignorance and sloppiness, greed and ugliness. Things were not as expected, when he remembered telling of plans to leave home territory and journey west to see what could be found. He would not guess on seeing a lot of unpleasantness; stuff that was neither beautiful nor wonderful, not important or worthwhile.

On his last day, Rudi was back at the ocean, a little further up the coast at another sailboat moorage. He met up with old school chums and a girl they knew, for one more thing he wanted to do before thinking of returning home. They were on a catamaran, heading west on the Pacific Ocean, for an evening sail. It was sunny and clear; three men and a woman, young people out after working, for a short adventure. The water was deepest blue but rippled on the surface to indicate fresh wind; enough sporting action for new friends. Going out was a happy scene: soaring seagulls swooping down to review their craft, hard white sails pulling them over a wide ocean and good companions at light banter. But they had to turn round, eventually. It was not a circle route or scenic tour -- simply a straight sail out, one tack away and another tack back home.

"Take the helm, Rudi, it's your turn" and one man went forward to deal with the lines; the girl changed sides and grabbed another line to pull, while the third man grabbed the main boom to bring across the cockpit. Everything started well, for the return distance; they knew the drill and enjoyed the unexpected. But the wind was falling as night approached, the sun was lowering fast and they had no auxiliary power. Birds had abandoned them, the water became flat and dark and ominous clouds began to pile-up like smoke from a stack. The fun was over -- now it was a race back to the harbor before the sails collapsed and the boat lost motion.

"I see landfall" said Rudi at last, "straight ahead, we're on course"!

It was completely dark by then, except the piers had lights and glass windows at the shoreline reflected the very last rays of sun behind them. The wind departed to the west where they found it and three long paddles were brought out to use at each side of the hull, as they edged towards safety. Rudi was pleased, because they were really proving themselves together, as their craft went straight ahead to the entrance. But the girl shouted out about the swell; how it was rising at the tidal bar and breaking at the entrance into a mass of turbulence. After making a little more distance Rudi saw a wall of black water rise behind them, many feet higher above the deck, like it was angry and vengeful; to menace and threaten them, overpower and swamp the small boat in one large crashing action.

"Okay, paddle hard, let's go" they heard "hold on tight"!

Turning forward Rudi did just as he was told; learned hard against an upright near him and panicked inside. There was a mighty big crash of water, like it became very heavy all of a sudden, smashing against everything in its path. Yet no one failed, the crew kept going; the craft stayed upright and was still moving. This same wave continued past them, to run-up against the beach; it was unconcerned about winning or losing, breaking or hurting anything or anyone. Only a few minutes later they followed and eventually went alongside the dock. Rope lines went out quickly to secure them. But two paddles were missing and a wind jacket; rails at the rear were bent and three grown sailors were grinning at the woman --

The next morning Rudi was meant for returning home and report to his father; always ready to hear about travels and life away from domestic confines. He was not disappointed, because like himself Rudi was a good raconteur, who liked to exaggerate and embellish his tales. The essential kernel, the basis of the stories he told, were true and worthwhile; with enough good humour to make them laugh out loud.

CHAPTER TEN

She was a young native Indian, shopping in the supermarket and went round-an-round the aisles filling her basket with all the essentials. But when she got to the cashier her credit was rejected and she had to leave the food stuff at the checkout.

"My brother had my bank stuff" she said.

"Maybe you can phone him" said the other lady. "Just outside, there's a pay-phone"!

There was a young man behind them, watching and listening, because she was a pretty girl in an awkward situation. He followed outside and saw her make a call, then wait at the kerbside. After the man took care of his own groceries, she was still waiting, looking up-an-down the traffic lanes. He felt some sympathy as it was near dinner time, time to eat. But she left her food in the store and had no money. So he walked over and asked to help –

"It's okay, he will come, my brother". She was embarrassed with his offer, yet managed to talk, about getting a new job and staying in a new place. Her own tribe was in the north, hundreds of miles away, so she was without family or friends here. Except for this one brother who borrowed her bank cards, who had a vehicle and was meant to show at front of the supermarket; so's they could buy groceries. The man did not like to see a girl stranded like this, a long way from home and trying to cover-up for a wayward sibling --

"D'you think he's coming" he asked?

"He wants to eat, but can't cook anything, so has to find me" she answered.

By then the girl was thinking the man was too concerned, too interested; she did not really want the attentions of a 'whiteman'. It was awkward and confusing; hoping he would go away before her brother showed, she began to shorten the conversation with abrupt responses and furtive looks. The man knew his intentions were ambiguous, so left her at front of the store and returned to his own *vehicle. Inside the front seat he glanced at the traffic lanes, to watch for other vehicles, but none came. She was still out there, waiting, when he slipped the brake and left the parking lot for the roadway, thinking to go on home –*

NEXT TWO EXITS

After Easter Rudi arranged to meet a friend from England and give him a grand tour, of sorts, in the Americas. Ray had written a few times, then telephoned his last details for the sojourn, to make it easy for them. Ray was not really a friend, but friend of a friend; desperate to savour some Western lore and to see for himself. Rudi was happy with the idea, because he usually got on well with different kinds. Instead of travelling for new places and new people, this time the new person was coming over to him. Then th-shoe would be on th-other-foot, so to speak; odd queries and searching comments would come at him, not the other way around. The next few days they spent a lot of time together; swapping stories about their pal and what Rudi planned for them. His first idea was to get into a vehicle and they see some of the country; a simple idea of seek and find, look and marvel, share and talk. A half-day journey took them into the mountains; a good choice for any tenderfoot or newcomer. It was hot and first chance they got was to find a creek and take a dip into clear soothing water, like it was pre-ordained and waiting for them.

Rudi had two companions all of a sudden; because he also saw an Indian boy at the creek, ready to dive and swim. It was his creek and his area, no arguing the way the boy stood poised on the rock, so Rudi could understand how this was not an unknown place. Ray was already in the creek, splashing the brown water over his shoulders and rubbing it over his face with happy fingers. But it was a fast creek and dangerous -- the way water rushed by the stones with great force in deeper parts and bottom sands shifted under the feet when

Rudi tried to balance and step out. Pulling with his left hand he got some fingers into the stones and took a deep breath, because he had fallen into the creek middle and was swept away. When he got low in the water, it did not pull so hard; he could cross his hands over and move sideways. He was swept over two more ledges in the creek bed, before gaining the bank to regain control. Stepping out onto dry rock and standing up straight in afternoon sun, he could find his balance; his position as young man out in summer, in the mountains, on holiday. He wanted to see the whole picture that day, like he always did --

The boy knew well how to go against the stream and be free with currents. He dived from fifteen feet to impress the visitors, then swam the narrow parts, to go against a speeding current. Rudi stood-up high nearby, seeing Ray trying to climb out and had to shout: "look at him go, no fear at all and he could have been alone today"!

"But we couldn't be much help", said Ray as he gained firm ground to stand and also watch a shy native boy at his proud play. He must have taken-a-shine to the two friends and wanted to show how it was up the canyon, how he came to master the dangers -- "We catch trout here; full of brown fish for weeks" he said. "I get plenty out the water as they crowd the small pools". This boy was pure and clean, strong and fresh, just like the water he swam in.

"Look, big bottom fish"! He talked of catching them with a small net. Rudi had to believe him after seeing his stellar performance that day. He was about fourteen, handsome and thoughtful -- just how Rudi wanted Ray to see this boy; how a lot of Indian boys were better away from town, away from school. Boys like this braved the creek for hundreds of years and fish returned to the spawning grounds of the upper reaches for a thousand years. No denying the heritage of the place and how it worked for the best. Ray had to leave town comforts and camp in the canyon to see the real country, like it was before more people came, before it could be spoiled.

It was a hot summer, by the time July came around and Rudi was full of things to do, for both of them. There was a big water inlet, not far from camp, which went back into the mountains for many miles. On the leeward side of the lake a deep cove became a known appendage, for boat moorage and swimming beach. Behind a small yacht club, there was a rental place for Indian canoes and kayaks, open all summer long.

The second time Ray went out in a canoe, Rudi insisted it was safe and essential for any visitor, as premium adventure for summer. So at nine-am they headed up the mountain lake with ready gear, like flasks of coffee, extra clothing and sandwiches. It was to be a straight route up the lake, till past noon, then round and back to the rental sheds before dark. Paddles were worked by the shoulders to keep them upright, Rudi tried to tell Ray, as the visitor leaned over to put his weight into it. When they got out of sight and alone on the inlet, the water became rough and wind came up behind them. Rudi became unsure about their course of action, but not soon enough to stop the open canoe going over, a half-mile from shore and above the deepest stretch of water. It was a sudden shock and two fools grasped the side of the craft as their predicament became clear: no help in sight, sheer rock at the shore and their belongings beginning to float-off in another direction. Life-vests made it safe, but nothing else was right; nothing they could do to save the day. It was already too serious to allow them any fear and they were winded enough to stop any panic. Though Rudi usually enjoyed clear blue water; today it was also cold and unfeeling with homicidal potential. Ray kept asking Rudi if he stood up to make it tip-over and asked again when Rudi swam after their personal gear seen floating away. Seemed like they made a mistake alright, difficult to explain and impossible not to feel stupid. It was now three-pm and a clear day in July, with enough time and space for them to think of something clever. But at four-pm the canoe went over again and they were very tired but not angry. No one had stood up or done anything foolish; it was just two wobbly bums in an Indian-style canoe, soft and untrained, weak and unstable.

Swimming went better; they were out in the water for less time and always closer to the shore. Of course they got bored with just one place and took to finding new beaches in Rudi's vehicle. Sometimes they made a whole day's journey to find a long lost cove, to purvey quiet seclusion with pristine water. They were more successful at swimming together, looking for eats together and had an interesting ferry ride to an old logging town, to see a piece of authentic heritage Rudi liked to brood over. They jumped on the ferry first-thing one morning and stood look-out on the top deck along the railings like ole-time explorers, to study the evolving views coming toward them from the western horizon.

Eventually, Rudi and his companion also went further inland away from the ocean; to explore the rivers and their settlements -- back into their vehicle. They made a good team like this: to ask the right questions, to find the helpful strangers and spur each other onward into the unknown. The two of them squirmed in the front seats for two more hours, because no place to stop, to see a lot more of the canyon. Ray could see how the valley became a canyon and the river course was stronger -- no more bottom fields to grow farm produce and no boats up this far. They both looked from opposite windows; Rudi saw to the left, front and rear. Ray looked right, across the canyon over to the blue-grey rock and clumps of green, the visitor's view of Indian territory up-state and north-west --

"Look over there" said Ray and "look at that"!

"This is a pulp mill and that is a log boom" Rudi said.

"What's that" Ray asked, "the sign -- Spuzum band Office"?!

"Spuzum Indians, reservation lands. They got to have an office" said Rudi.

"Why an office up here? What's the need"!

"To make coffee, of course. Further back is a 'long house' to make talk, peace talk and such like – get it"!

Their vehicle was sturdy enough to keep going, for sufficient speed and easy conversation -- till they made another stop-over. They had a ready walk-out from a parking space to the entrance; pausing on the lot to stand-an-stretch for a few observation comments. When a tall Indian man appears, Rudi asks "is there another cafe further up the canyon"?

"What's wrong with this place"?! He stops to pull out his arms and insists upon it. Rudi swings back to counter -- "nothing, nothing wrong with this place" he shouts out bringing Ray round to his flank. When the three men come into line they head through the door as new-found friends, to find a clean vacant table. The Indian man sides off to a window to look out and smoke, finished with talking; while another man comes infront of Rudi and Ray with noisy talk and glasses of water.

"Hi there, what you got"?

"To drink, you mean – too hot to eat, eh"!

"We came all the way from the coast this morning and glad to stop".

"I never go there, but my wife moved back to town, because she's a party girl; our daughter is with us". He went-on a bit more about his wife, a daughter and his father at the window seat.

"Where is she; my friend here, is a teacher? Let's see her".

"Over at her friend's yard, swimming".

Rudi explained to Ray how this was a Dutch half-breed; a handsome man who enjoyed talking, the white side; but had a good family round him, the Indian side. Rudi made more of his anthropology breakdown between comments on the salad and tea they had. Ray concentrated on the hot tea because he thought it cooled him, while Rudi chomped the green salad with both drinks equally. He lorded it over Ray with his bush-craft, his sign reading and gave the signal to move off.

"My turn to pay, here, let's go".

The café man then became the cashier so that Rudi had to grab him on the arm, holding against his chest, to make a real good-bye. It was enough for them to talk over the next hour; to make connections between this reservation and Indians Ray saw in town, not forgetting a boy at the river. "It's beginning to make sense" he said. "I see, okay; I get what you mean, Rudi, amazing"!

"Sure; you'd do the same for me in London, Ray -- thanks". They

114

had to be equal and kept a good balance between them for the weeks they were together; because they were both same level up their own totem poles. They were now over a hundred miles out from home. Yet it was very compelling to keep going; up-higher, further-out, further-away and on towards the night like they had a schedule to meet; though dusk was clearly descending upon the road ahead. Before they finally stopped to turn and head back Rudi was speeding up, as if to catch the moment of return further away; a few more miles up the road grade, round just one more rock bluff --

"Let's walk out a bit, before we start again" said Ray, like Rudi would say.

"Yeah, a'course we will" echoed into the dim dusk air and he leaned against the hood, after three steps out the vehicle. Ray traversed the black-top to the road-side growth and back to the other line of brush, now darkening its greenery to the falling light, eventually satisfied with something.

On the way home, Rudi went into another roadside café, after he dropped Ray off. He needed time to himself before turning-in for the night. It was a very ordinary place, the way he liked it and quite, empty. A young lady was attending the tables this time, broadly built with two strong plaits in her dark hair and red ribbons for effect. She lingered at his table with her towel and held onto a wide smile for a long time; while her customer chewed his way through cake and then grabbed onto his mug of tea.

"Is that all" she kept saying, "anything more"?

But he couldn't find any answer and fumbled with the food, poked at his tea-bag in the pot with the spoon and started to yawn.

It was an Indian gal in the café, just off the reserve and he another 'Whiteman' on the move, with lots to leave behind and lots to hide. He managed to spy upon her as she saddled across the floor to other customers and liked what he saw; thought she was happy and willing, maybe willing to make him happy. But time for bed, he mused -- no more distractions and no more play.

The night before Ray had to return home, they had a traditional

115

evening session in a western bar. It was meant to be icon of the western states, as something big for Ray to remember. "Come to England, Rudi; visit me in London. I owe you a favour -- for a great holiday".

"Okay then – start with another round of ale, first, can yuh"?

"For sure".

"And some roasted nibble things for us. What's it like"?

"What's that"!

"What's London like, where you live? I read about England once; some Robin Hood stories, up in Nottingham"!

"I live in Earls Court, Kensington town. Come and visit next summer; see for yourself".

"But summer is good here"!

"Said I owed you a favour, forget about round here, just for one year".

"A year"!

"I mean one summer. Take a'look round a big city -- really different to America -- be good for you"!

"Maybe! You got any apple-pie over there and is the beer cold enough? How about that round of ale you promised"!

Rudi paid more attention when Ray went up to buy and was concerned about going away, all of a sudden, the pressure to promise something like that. Rudi thought to visit Mexico again; but England was across another ocean, further than New York City.

Ray was trying to swagger at the bar counter and make casual with his order, like a real westener. He returned with two bottles, two chip packets and a big sigh as he regained his soft seat, to eat and drink with two hands. He sat opposite Rudi but looked elsewhere; across a long darkened room that reeked of smoky ale and stale talk, coming to ten-pm.

"What's this, ole stick"?

"Corn chips and Irish ale. Try it, like mother's milk, don't you know"!

"It's very black"!

"Irish stout is like black velvet".

"I only want a drink, Ray; I ain't here for health or illumination. A'just need a drink tonight".

"Why"?

"For saying good-bye; the best way I know how".

The bar was filling-up the usual way for Sunday evening, irregular drinkers and noisy with it; while Rudi searched the face of Ray to see where he'd fit in with London town. Ray was very flat-faced to the force of the place and kept at his talk like no one was there except Rudi and himself; no one else hearing, listening, within earshot. This was a further concern for Rudi, to think of a serious trip overseas, when sometimes he could not fathom his companion.

Quite the opposite of Thetis Island, he was thinking of last year – very open and accommodating. It was way over on the west coast, up a long reach of water into an old logging site; where a café-store combination stood with boats at a small marina. Two teenage girls attended the lunch counter to talk about school on the next island. They also talked about college in another town on the mainland and glanced across the water to a horizon on the bay, to see a promising light for them passing behind the charcoal clouds.

"Any more coffee"?

"I had enough, thankyou. Which way to the ferry"?

"It's already gone! Nothing now till four o'clock".

"Today"?

"Yeah – there's two ferries a day; except on Saturday there's only one and no ferries on Sunday".

"What about national holidays and such, like Christmas"?

"Same as Sunday" she said.

Rudi took the joke far enough and decided to get up and leave, before it got awkward, before she saw how he was fooling her.

The walk back of the residence led to a road, a gravel track, to find the ferry harbour a mile away. There was a pub-style shack at the gates; but Rudi wanted to keep walking after he saw the clientele through the windows, looking seedy and unhappy. The woods were different with lots of clean air; light gently filtering through the fir trees and the trails nicely paved with wood chips. Rudi kept at walking and followed a track up a hill and down to more waterline, with a lot of still silence; his breath vaporizing in the clean air and the wildlife keeping a safe distance out-of-sight –

It was months later, when Rudi wrote a letter to his pal in London, long after the weather changed and he stayed indoors a lot more --

"-- greetings from the Wild West. Remember what I told you about us! September, began a year of Humanity study at the college I mentioned. A full year of philosophy, history, literature, till next May. So will not be coming to England like you thought -- thanks anyway. You made a good offer. I like to travel we know that and went to Mexico for three months; can say a lot more in Spanish. I love the Pacific Ocean down there and got an appetite for tamale pie and DosXXX beer. How-ma doing so far, mate?!

Went fishing last chance I got, four grown salmon and a catfish; using the rod and line you left behind, lucky for me I guess. No, I don't throw catfish back, in case I catch it again. I get rid of 'em permanent..

Tell me more about Earls Court -- the way you write in stylish English. Is it a court yard or near a court house and who was Earl? Real interesting place you must live -- tell me more. Please do. Your ole pal -- Rudolph Borah.

P.S. any good fishing over there"?

"Rudi -- sorry not to reply of late -- urgent errands to attend. The West is out of mind now; I battle local wolves at my door, taxes and creditors and public nuisances... Glad to get your letter though, or it would seem like a dream I had over there; please keep in touch. Lots of Yanks arrive every Easter at the nearby subway station; you can fall in with them if you get shy. I know you get terribly shy sometimes; so unusual in a grown man these days. See you next year 'partner', when the ground thaws and I go to the corner block to scout my district for strangers and such --

R.M.

n.b. sorry, no fish or game over here"!

It turned out, the following year Rudi had a new partner who also liked swimming and discussing the big issues; like where people came from and why they were different.

"D'you think it's hotter today, more than yesterday"? When he raises his head off a towel roll. "D'you think those two are the same ones over there"?

"Who"?

"Same girls we swam with, the day before, at the boat jetty"?

"Could be".

"Are they Indian gals, Rudi; looks like to me"? Up on his elbows now, gazing towards where he said.

"No, they're not Indians; not from round here, that's for sure. Asian ladies, I'd say. A whole bunch in the city last year, students and the like".

"Look the same to me, same as the ones at the jetty, same as Indians".

"No, they're not".

"Same hair and colour, same features"!

"Yes, the same racial origin, apparently. Did you know our Indians came from Asia, by way of the Alaska landbridge, then southward; over eight thousand years ago? But seems our Indians became 'Red Skins' and the Asians stayed 'yellow'"!

"Ha-ha"!

"Now there's no connection anymore; the land-bridge has gone and the ones we got don't like commerce while the others love that money paper. Our natives don't love money or paper, they love fishing and drinking, or dancing and traveling"!

"What about swimming and eating"?

"That's us, yuh talking about us again. Give me the flask please; you reminded me of something" --

The two Asian girls stood on a rock shelf a hundred yards away and dried in the sun; towelling their hair and wet shoulders/arms. They were talking a lot and basking in warm air, uncaring of admiring eyes; wanting to be seen at their best on a fine afternoon at the inlet. Rudi could see the talking but not hear it; could guess it was very foreign; as heads shook with the words and arms/hands moved in short strokes to underline the text of a conversation. Quite different to Rudi and his distracted responses, the way loose movement followed his sentences. His companion was different again, preferring to remain still when speaking -- "I want to talk with the girls, see where they come from, like what you said"!

All sorts of folk enjoyed visiting the West those days and Rudi was usually a good host, polite too, if they were engaging females. He liked to think he was going to become a man's man someday. But in the meantime, he heard a lot of different ideas about that; so it became confusing for him, when he was often isolated and sometimes very stubborn.

CHAPTER ELEVEN

Girls from the café decided upon a birthday party for their visitor from out of town and helped the lawyer cook a special dinner in his funky apartment, up in North Beach, on Washington Square. They cooked meat in the oven and steamed vegetables on the stove, to be served with European beer they bought on way up the street, mostly for the benefit of his pal. One of the younger gals dug out a party-hat for him. She found a ten-gallon stetson above his closet, a Navy cap, then a flight helmet he used in the aircraft. On the front it said, 'Lt. Kennedy' and he grinned at the memories produced; wearing it at the table and laughing out loud. He now sported a red beard with modest ponytail, because he was an attorney in the city; but hip, enjoying the alternative lifestyle. Altogether it was a comical scene and appeared to put military service a long way behind him.

America was changing after the Vietnam War and veterans were not regarded the same as before -- "I served over the Antarctic ice-cap, from our fleet carrier, based in New Zealand" he explained. "We had our sledge dogs sat in the cabin, tied, so they would not crap everywhere -- but I was navigator, up front". The food was very good, so that his friends were too busy eating, to listen. But the girls were admiring a real trooper, encouraging him; pushing hot food into his whiskers and sitting close by.

AFTER HOURS

When a young man leaves home and uses his automobile to reach new places, he often gets more than he bargained for. Rudi Borah was on the road for years and had to contend with a few upsets along the way, the least expected; lots of round-th-corner surprises waiting for him. But he had talents, to share, like an interest in music and sport. First, he had to pay for things. Happily, Rudi was a country boy, so any job was acceptable for a while --

Rudi took the night shift for another week, for a personal favour. He needed to have friends at work, because it was useful and more secure. He did not know how the risk went up at night, when predators might appear after dark – in the country or in town. During August the nights were warm enough to make for pleasant duty; the sky was dark, but sent drafts of warm air across the town, as far as his station on Soquel Avenue. Rudi began washing the floors of the garage by one-am, after replacing the bench tools into wall brackets and emptying garbage containers round the back. He parked his jacket in the office and loosened his uniform shirt; to enjoy the quiet time and empty thoughts, like he always did. Two seagulls suddenly arrived at signposts at front of the lot, where they settled on the tops, close together. He wondered why they did not sleep on pylons at the harbour, lots of good places along the marina; yet these two appeared happy with the posts at his gas station. They both looked round over the lot to feel safe, before turning heads back into their feathers.

At the same time a dusty sedan arrived at the farthest pumps, as if to be unnoticed; the lights went off and then the engine. Two men in the front seat waited till Rudi walked over to them; when one got out and lit a cigarette, while the other started talking: "Fill her up, will you son"?

"Yes Sir".

"And it needs oil; we came a long way today".

"No need to tell him anything".

"What's the harm, Al, he's just a kid".

"I said no names"!

"Maybe he's a bright kid at that".

"No Sir, not really".

"Don't protest so much, you give yourself away. I can see you're a clean-cut college type. It's alright, we mean no harm".

"Shut it, Mack, shut it will yah"!

The air became heavy and dense all of a sudden; not like sunny California, more like Chicago or Detroit, crowded and industrial.

Rudi felt he was now in a big wicked city, not a small beach town; feeling a bit chilly and exposed. But he had to defuse the tension and walked away to the garage before returning to the engine hood and the oil stick. There was a strain in the air, an awkwardness; yet he could not see why, or what he could do about it on his own. Rudi glanced up at the signposts, no change there; just two tired birds sleeping through the sore business of men, their heads buried deep into neck feathers.

"Say, what's your name, kid"?

"It's Rudi".

"Okay lad, the oil is good and we have a full tank. We gotta go. Nice meeting you and good luck".

"He sure has luck, Al".

"I already told you once, Mack, quiet"!

"Thankyou, Sir".

They went off away as quickly as they came. The ole-style sedan started-up noisily and turned into the lane, onwards like it slid on rails, gone. Then the seagulls took their cue to awake and began calling out, as if there was a connection between them Rudi could not know about, as if the two gulls and two men were one and the same.

Rudi had work to finish; he had to catch-up and get ready to leave for home. He was spooked alright, but was it real or only phantoms of the dark, ghosts of the night. Sometimes ordinary things became distorted at night-time; especially when alone every night, dreaming of a shift change. But no time to figure it out, when he had an arrangement next day, to meet-up with a local luminary. She was linked to the new symphony orchestra gathered together in town and her husband an executive in the recording business. Contrary to her stated plan the lady decided to hurry their lunch and directed Rudi out the café back to her house; explaining how the orchestra was barely constituted and how her role was advisory.

There were three men already in the living room, when Rudi came into the house. This was not a normal suburban scene, because a record player was turned-up loud and center-stage in the living room, with an older man at the volume control. He was close to the floor speakers and leaning over a little.

"This is John Coltrane" he said and passed the album sleeve over to Rudi. It said, 'A Love Supreme' on the cover, above a tall black man on a saxophone, all in black-an-white. Rudi was trying to understand the man, the music and this context; but it was difficult –

"You are European stock, my wife said. So no jazz, eh"?

"Well" --

"No 'black' Jazz, that's for sure"!

"Honey, this is Rudi. We just came from an 'alternate' café in town, you know the place". The man was paying more attention to the speakers, not really listening to her, the keen attention of a long time devotee. He was moving, swinging at his place and humming along – like an epiphany was happening for him, a close encounter with the sublime – his features blanched, eyes half-closed and fingers clicking at his sides. It was not a good time to talk –

"Edward, have some tea; please give this to our guest". Not a good time to ask. The other two guests were also standing, equal distance apart, adjacent to the turntable; young local boys about Rudi's age. They were studiously silent and still – undecided about the music or confounded with the situation; though appreciative of the sax sounds coming from expensive speakers, hosted by a musical elder. Their connection with the man was unclear, but not their interest in music.

Rudi wanted out now, he wanted to hear more of Coltrane or anything about him, but not today. There seemed to be some serious family business brewing over alcohol and frustration, anger and disappointment from the lady, reverberating from the man.

"Misses Moran, I must go – got lots on today".

"You leaving so soon"?!

"We'll see you again; don't worry".

"Alright Rudi. You can come over any time, right dear"? Her husband could not respond, in the middle of some very strong riffs, not even to glance over.

Rudi departed the set and nothing changed, no one moved – except that Coltrane was rushing through a whole package of sound and mood, rhythm and tone – the long-playing disc kept going round and round, no one wanted to stop that. Rudi's leaving was not so important, no surprise, nothing like the wife inferred. When the front door opened, sounds leaked out of confines; it was somehow difficult to pull the door shut, after the saxophone got free of the house. Rudi succeeded, by making a slow firm action with the brass handle and went quickly to the sidewalk, as good escape into town. Yet the music lasted a long time for him; quite apart from the unsettling circumstance he strayed into.

Unlike music, sport was more straight forward, more direct; like young men normally preferred. Rudi played field games at school and liked to swim the creeks in summer – but professional 'boxing' was a big draw for all men, because it was real; to show strength and courage, pluck and luck.

The big fight was to be held in Las Vegas, another state, but aired live on TV screens around the country. He had enough time-off work, for the favours he did his pals and made his way to a popular 'watering hole'. It was a bout between a known champion and unlikely contender so that Rudi arrived at the pub early for once, to rush past the doors and pay his ticket. It was a strip-tease joint, mid-town and down market for basic service of beer and girls, food and music – but not tonight. Rudi could see over a hundred men gathered in the place, same as any Saturday night, except there were hardly any ladies. One or two did take the stage, strutting their stuff as usual, before the viewing screens were switched on. But no one took any notice this time; absolutely no men in the stage seating or sitting anywhere near. The girls kept at it, dancing and calling out to the men, but to no avail. They were preoccupied elsewhere, not even to peek over their shoulder, as skimpy clothing was unshed with much flair and fanfare – it did not matter, not tonight. The club bouncer was a man in his prime, tall and heavy, enough to be good at his job; tossing people out the door if they drank too much or they grabbing at the girls. Tonight he was greatly changed, quiet at the door for the tickets; then he wandered the floor like a greeter would, chatting to everybody and shaking hands.

"Have a nice night; should be a great fight" he exclaimed to Rudi when they crossed paths at the bar.

"Yeah, you too"! It was strange for Rudi to be friendly with the big man; who normally scowled and stomped round the tables in full view, like his job required. Lots of extra chairs were available, grouped near the TV monitors and the men quickly became friends, making hand-shakes and talking out. Anticipation was high and had nothing to do with alcohol, because few men managed to buy a glass of beer, in the rush to get seated. Rudi sat infront of his group, but kept his shoulders down and let his head slope forward, for the benefit of those behind. "Thankyou", they called out and friendships just kept going. During the contest Rudi was struck how they all seemed to react together, like the applause was synchronized and calling out often got a quick follow-up, a clever response that was also humorous like it had been scripted. Testosterone and hormones were not always about aggression or fighting, like they said; more likely for kindred spirits and cameradie. It was surprising to see the changed behaviour and men directing their attention towards other men. This was something the women could not understand, did not enjoy; highlighting the special occasion for male patrons that night. 'Men without women' was not a new theme and Rudi read all about it long before he left home, took a job, bought a vehicle, or kissed a girl.

A week later Rudi was back to the alternate café and trying to catch-up on his educational credentials, classical music this time. Someone had donated an old gramophone to play, for the benefit of patrons and staff alike. Rudi sat twiddling his spoon on the saucer when the next LP was dropped onto the turntable, as everyone waited for Chopin and his piano pieces, the 'Polonaises'; straight into the deep-end for a country boy removed to a college town. They were three more people at his table with food infront, drinks and conversation. But for a while Chopin took over the scene; his keyboard notes in big major chords, strong enough to make everyone stop to hold their breath, as new rhythms were heard and new moods entered the equation.

"I thought we got this before", looking over to the staff station, as if to inquire?

"That was last week, lad".

"You need to know this piece, Rudi".

"Why"?

"To impress the ladies".

"Not easy to forget the thumping of keys and pounding rhythms – more like a military march, I'd say".

"Well, gals like soldiers too"!

Rudi was looking round to see other customers distracted and caught off-balance with the café music. This was definitely not 'white noise', lounge sounds, or radio pabulum to smooth your feathers and get folks talking, eating and spending. This sound was not trying any of that stuff – something else – getting your attention first-off. Other patrons in the room were experiencing the same and turning in their seats; glancing about and pausing in speech, in thought. No denying the power of the music: threatening and confounding the way the pace accelerated and seemed to be so forceful for everyone.

"I have to go" said one "it's my cue to get to class; Victorian Lit at the college"!

"No excuses needed", said the lawyer at the table, "it gets very loud".

The same album played twice more that week and again the next week, before Rudi was told about the bias; a new employee was Polish and fancied himself composing. Of course everyone was in benefit with such resurrections from the concert halls of ole Europe and the café crowd were liberal towards anything classical or anything foreign. Rudi knew how vocals now led the way with American music; new kinds of singing to bring new kinds of song to

127

the public. The piano never led anymore, like it did before, in old time Warsaw. Hearing the various pieces was a bit of a history lesson, Rudi discovered, when he read about Chopin on a library visit. He thought about how Vienna and Paris must have been a kool place way back then; a bit like the 'village' in New York or like San Francisco. Everyone in the café seemed to feel the same as Rudi, because he could sense no rancor or disquiet, when the album ran on towards a crashing crescendo at the end of each piece.

"Me too" said Rudi, "gotta work in the morning".

"Goodnight, then, fella"!

"Bye". They all signaled permission for him to leave, when they nodded or flicked up a hand. Rudi had been among new found friends all evening, like attending a fashionable salon in Paris or Berlin, though he hardly knew their names. On the way home he took to heavy breathing, to vapourize some of his cares and dreams. It was to be a long day of work ahead next morning, with no music, less friends and many more demands.

A few weeks later, Rudi got off work for the afternoon to see boxing again and went over to Second Street by one o'clock. He paid two dollars at the door and went upstairs to the old-style gym, of pre-war interest from the 'dirty thirties', when pugilism was a popular escape from unemployment. From the stale surroundings he encountered, it was easy to imagine desperate men turning another cheek to a training partner and rising early to run the empty streets. There was an uncommon group of American blacks this time, reporters and sundry; making for a lot of people on the street and at the doorway entrance to a run-down gym facility. But there was also excitement in the air, something new and important happening for once, in a forgotten district. Two prized fighters would be on the premises today and a small entrance ticket would allow a long view of the session. Muhammad Ali was fighting George Chuvalo the next week and this was a prelim event for the media and the aficionados, to see how the two men squared-off.

Rudi got there early, before the main contender and he saw

Chuvalo chasing a sparing partner round the ring; angry and powerful against a smaller man defended in head-gear, kidney protection and jock-strap. George was loud and aggressive, looking very scary for everyone; a convincing show for the press and trainers alike. Then Ali showed-up and began causing a lot of commotion at the door and up the stairs. The day's training was divided in halves, but they crossed paths in the middle, when Ali let out a tirade of verbal abuse against George. The rest of the time Ali was quiet and studious, working hard at the exercises, then chatting quietly with his family. A young black woman sat close by with a small child, to watch the proceedings and talk with their famous father.

Ali was quite the athlete; astounding the gathering with his rope-skipping, when sweat did not so much run down his body, it exploded off his torso like a boiling kettle. Shadow boxing in the ring followed and sweat splashed into pools on the canvas from inside his jerkin, when it was lifted between the three-minute rounds. Ali also chatted amicably, without effort for reporters and such like, on top of his furious practise at the punching ball. Rudi could see he was no taller than himself and slightly built compared to Chuvalo; but he was mighty fit and set to triumph. There were more black men round the arena, looking like club touts from Los Angeles and Rudi tried to talk with them.

"Is that enough training" he said, after a two hour stint concluded? "It seems a bit short"!

"He's winding down for the fight" – the black man replied.

"Why's that" – to admit some ignorance and engage conversation?

"The big training was months ago, man! What d'you know"!? The man with snappy white-trim round his hat, was irritated by this dumb honky. He kept glancing away, deliberately, in way of sending a message.

"Okay, thanks, I got it" Rudi added, trying to justify himself. But the black man did not respond, except to nod his head up-an-down in jaunty fashion; like he was still in the ghetto, for home boys only. Naïveté and curiosity did not always sit well with people and racial attitudes could work both ways; this was at least fair, in America, the land of opportunity. 'Race' was still a constant feature all over America, no escaping it really, when native Indians first took 'white men' into their realm; to be followed by other aliens, desirable or not.

At another time Rudi was taking a ride across town with a different kind of friend; he was a bit older and enjoyed a vehicle to be lazy. There were two of them in the front seats, on Saturday morning, end of the week and they free of obligations and such --
"What's that"?
"Black vocals"!
"Yeah" – it was awkward, when colour seemed to be the issue again, instead of the music.
"But who"?
"Rawls – you saying yuh never heard of Lou Rawls"?!
There was a brown syrupy vocal on the car radio, infront of them – and there was colour in the music, a dark tone, along with a slow beat you would think to get in the southern states.
"Yes – No. Well, I heard his name and saw his poster up at the bookstore".
The rhythm was clearly amorous and warm; the words were pop pabulum and smooth for easy intake. There was sweetness and temptation in the chat which followed each song, between Lou and the callers phoning-in to the radio station. But there was no message/content, none that Rudi could savvy; it was simply intimacy and radio technology at a new interface; a young black vocalist reaching out to black and white alike, females mostly. Rudi also found it irresistible and an undeniable blend of sex/sound and proximity/privacy within a moving vehicle in the city; like a sexual encounter on the back seat of a coup, where confinement added to the mix. Rudi could sense that Lou knew his listeners well and the kind of venue they favoured, not really the drawing room or the concert hall.
"Yeah, alright, it sounds good", trying to appreciate the

performance, without losing the kool response required from the driver; because it was not Rudi's automobile, not his radio.

"How about eating, somewhere, you dig"!? – as Lou continued with his sweet rap and the next song. Yet they were all much the same. He had some success in the Bay Area that summer and clearly set to continue this popular trend, before he had to think of new material. The radio speakers still tuned to the singer were loathe to let go, when the car turned into a parking lot behind a café outlet.

"You want lunch, or breakfast"?

"Not till Lou is finished; I can't eat until then", was an impressive answer. The full 'bars' of west coast crooning continued as if nothing happened for them; till the driver forgot how the music would also die when he cut the engine ignition. Rudi never ate breakfast out before he got to California; where he saw lots of breakfast joints, with pairs of hungry folk at each window table; like they were contemplating the dawn or looking to see someone. Eventually, he went to eat like this on his own sometimes and deliberated over the kind of eggs he wanted, a good choice of toast; thinking of his parents back home in the kitchen. Did they miss him the same way he missed them at this time of day? Rudi was musing over this again; trying to decide if it was nostalgia for his home, his parents, or simply a weakness –

He drove his own vehicle out one day, in a hurry to leave work behind, leave all the loose-ends to someone else. It was parked in a lane, usually safe, because it would be close by. Just getting into his sedan, another auto started backing towards him and hit the right-side door – enough to dent the whole side, with paint falling off to reveal damaged metal. It was so sudden Rudi had no chance to prevent the mishap and then saw the other driver was a chauffeur. He stayed put while another man got out of the rear seats and stepped over to take a look. It was an old man, but he seemed to be tough and important; his car an expensive limousine. The man spoke slow and clear like he already knew something: "nice car you got, kid, is it your first"?

"Yeah it is; thanks".

"Well no need for insurance or anything like that. Maybe you could use some cash, a lot more. What'd'you say"?

"Sounds okay to me".

"Name your price, then". When Rudi suggested a round figure it was readily accepted and the man went back to his car. He said, "follow us and we can settle-up now, alright". Rudi got a few yards behind the limo and they both went slowly along the roads, like it was a small funeral procession. The lead vehicle finally pulled-up at back of a big restaurant and the old man went inside. The big pay-off was unexpected and set-up Rudi nicely for a trip home. But another stay off work might jeopardize his job, he thought, when striding onto the station lot next day to mumble about his plans to journey out-of-state and visit family; how he would definitely return to work, wanted to come back, could be relied upon and trusted like that. The boss looked back at him in uncommitted silence, before answering --

"When you thinking to leave, you say? Is it the weekend"?

"A Monday".

"Glad you still look-out for your parents. I have a son away in the Navy; but you know all about that".

The drive out-of-town to the state line was dull and routine; lots of stop-lights, traffic and the usual collection of roadside concessions with no good landscapes in view. When the road began to rise higher the terrain cleared and he could see for miles, see something worthwhile. That first night away he was fortunate and found a suitable place to stay, a low-cost motel, when darkness came. His vehicle pulled to a stop at an old style hitching rail at front and Rudi was glad to let the engine cool-off in the mountain air. His mood became a little rueful when the light faded ever so slowly, ever so gently. A crimson glow spilled onto everything from a flaming sky above, with yellow streaks across to give directions – like where the sun went to after dark and how to get home. It was a good omen for him, last thing at night; when he only needs to sleep before finding the highway again next morning. But Rudi had more friends to meet before re-acquainting with his own family at home.

132

There were two of them, a white man and native Indian. They were friends mostly because of the need; both down-an-out, out of luck, needing drinks and smokes. Rudi didn't have either, but he had a mite of sympathy and some free talk. They each got up several times, from squatting at the wall, to shake his hand firm and fair; then plopped down again in front of his room. The men were happy with Rudi as new-found friend and neighbour. Their two units were adjoining, so the Indian kept going into Rudi's place to look for ashtrays or drinking cups and Rudi at the front kept up a friendly chat. It felt like family for a short while, with three men joking and laughing/expiring; Rudi leaning/stretching back against his parked vehicle.

In a few minutes he would be under the blankets and dozing off, in a small room on the hillside, overlooking another hill and creek between them. It was a fitting end to the day, as it should be, because he was set to cover a lot of miles the next day. With his head on the pillow, barely a dream began, when sleep quickly descended and overpowered him.

CHAPTER TWELVE

Les was a devoted California surfer, with a difference. Every afternoon he took his surfboard to the bluff, just out of town; scaled down the rocky slope and entered the water behind a rising swell. His style was a bit stiff and his board an old Hawaiian product, which was big and heavy, made of timber; not modern fiber-glass. In the mornings he was journeyman printer for a local newspaper; then past noon he piled into his vintage Cadillac, with the old board protruding from the rear and went out to catch the breaking waves --

He was known as 'King Kong' of the surf, because Les was not young anymore and mostly bald on top. Rumours were he was already a grandfather and that he served with the Navy in World War-Two. After each run upon a cresting wave he paddled back beyond the swell with his young pals and started another ride to the beach. He got up at centre of the board, to be sure, crouching a little and focusing ahead. There were to be no tricks or showing-off for him; simply a straight try for the shore, like gliding in the sky or shooting a true arrow, to find the edge again. Balance and daring, skill and success were coming together in a very special way, one more time --

Occasionally, someone would shout over, to catch him off-balance: "hey, Les, wait for me"! But he enjoyed calling back to them: "can't talk now, kid, watch me go"!

THE FAMED PACIFIC

Someone wrote: 'to understand is the booby prize'; in other words, maybe not worth much. Rudi was reading a column in the newspaper, one quiet Sunday; a long warm morning for him to get comfortable and lazy. 'No good searching the rear-view mirror' it said, 'look infront and forward'. He kept on reading, to find a handle, to get a' hold of it. Rarely he tried editorials, preferring easy headlines and amusing trivia, after a full week of papers from his work; but the writing was sound. For a few moments he did look forward and infront as suggested, though it was difficult; then looked backwards through this mirror to go for the 'booby prize' he thought to have, that he now wanted. Maybe it was worth something; not worthwhile for anyone else, only for himself. His, a muddled career with lots of heartache and surprises; with work and travel to the fore. He did not really seek understanding, but simply enjoy a sepia version of how he got from there to here. This was very much his own life, making his mark; like the first cry tearing from a new born baby, strong and marvelous. Before college, before Rudi went professional, he took blue-collar employment in old style California, when he was young and lean; he still very young then and very lean --

It was at mid-day when two hungry work-mates sat together:
"Here, you can have my sandwich"!
"No time this morning, to get anything".
"I'm okay today; Rob is good to me, happy this week; so I fixed a lotta food for us".
"Not me, not okay – too loud in there, too warm and too dark; same every damn day". Rudi was migrant help for the season, in a new town, a new state. But he enjoyed slogging round in gumboots and denim, enjoyed a fabled work culture everyone respected.

She was an Asian girl, with husband and child; but needed to work in the San Cutraz cannery every day same as Rudi; to box field sprouts, clean, cut and size them for the market stores. Long lines of moving production tasks set out under big corrugated sheds, all week except for Sunday, down on Main Street. It was second break in their shift and they sat in the front seats of her truck, out on the company parking lot. Rudi had a drink in his lap, the girl with a lunch pail opened; but she never looked over to him while they talked.
"You can finish this, I got too much".
"Thankyou".
"You don't say much, really, but I like the quiet type. Rob likes to

136

be loud with his friends and laughs at me a lot. I don't mind, so long as I take care of him; like since we went together at San Cutraz High, since the beginning. And when I get old, when I die; I get to be buried beside him at the far side of town, next to my baby --

Take this, here, there's more --

I never had another boy at school, not even out of school; we met in summer classes and he was my first".

She went on like this for a long time while Rudi ate slowly and quietly, thinking how she saw love as some kind of end game, which seemed morbid. He always wanted love to be playful and friendly. Enjoying their comforts he let her go on, guessed it was better not to speak, that it was better to listen. This appeared to make her happy because she laughed in the telling, waved her arms about and chomped hard on her food; easy for Rudi like that, to let her hold forth every time. Every day they ate lunch like this together, not in the cafeteria, but in the privacy of her truck. David, his friend, warned Rudi not to eat with her, not be seen with her; unless he wanted to be shot by a jealous husband, or set upon by another man. How it was not good sense, would lead to trouble, everyone could see them together.

Later he did succeed in avoiding the gal, like David said and sneaked off to the company cafeteria to get some chili beans and thick bread; but was shy about this kind of trickery. So he sat alone at end of the bench trying to think about other things; about another part of America he knew from before and things for him to do after work. A whole week went by until the girl stepped infront of him, early one day: "were you ill, or something, I thought you had quit"!

His protestations were feeble and awkward, so he apologized a couple of times and went to sit with her again that day; so's she could continue telling him about Rob and something terrible. How he also had a lady friend at this same cannery, last year, had dates with her after work shifts -- his best friend told her. Rudi was worried about the obvious grudge. But said she could not do anything like that, because it was not the same for her; how she loved him and their child, because she never had another boy; never wanted another and was going to be buried next to him and that he was an Italian boy. Nothing more for Rudi to ask about, all pretty clear; how a gal got married out of school, got a baby, then first job. No college for her and no travelling like Rudi; no day-dreaming or loafing like some of his pals. Maybe she was happy, happy like an ignorant beast and Rudi the foolish one. Maybe she was more real, more honest and more loved; being with her each day like this made him think hard about it every time.

Of course there were many men on the job too, all kinds of men and one of the newly hired ones was very different from the girl and easier to be with. Johannes came to the cannery a month after Rudi started, but became prominent straight away; a few years older and just back from army service overseas in Vietnam, was married and said he had a baby. This was a lot of credential for everyone in the cannery, in a small town, down by the railway tracks; he made a strong impression. Johannes was playful, a bit of a 'joker' on the job. He took a long broom handle to his mouth, each break, to blow on it like a bugle horn and really make it sound out; everybody heard it and the foreman must have heard but turned a deaf ear. He also had funny things to say to the old ladies and made them laugh like girls. At the parking lot, where men gathered near the gates, Johannes went to take a big part without over playing his hand. Rudi thought he was looking at himself in the future, when he had more years at work, more time with men and travel under his belt and a lot more success with women.

"I don't care, if I ever make love again", Johannes said one day at a lull in the idle talk, "just don't care, because I had enough". It was wild talk, for any man, infront of young ones.

"Speak for yourself", someone yelled out!

"What about drink and smokes" yelled another?

"You had enough of that"!

But the lull continued, because they were stumped and caught off guard. Rudi was unsure if he really meant this or not. But just hearing it out loud was serious, enough to make him embarrassed as he was way behind with all this; behind with women, certainly not had nearly enough. Though he looked forward to saying this one day, like Johannes; like it could be a real goal for him to aim for.

Years before, Rudi started on a farm after school working with all the chores; moving onto construction sites, then into surveying work. He always took stock in his progress; took measure of his worth at each new venture and made friends for respect and interest. Rudi was sidelining another part of life, an important part, as if to catch-up later; friendships with women he decided to postpone, as if up to him alone, his own decision. But women did not want to disappear; why should they and they might enjoy creating distractions to confuse him and mislead. Such was Rosa, who wanted to use him against her own man friend, a risky plan for sure. She wanted something extra from her man; more worthwhile attention and seemed to believe that Rudi was sent to help out.

Rosa was already a bit of a bombshell at nineteen years old, with very proud bosom and long curly hair across her shoulders. She was new gal at the sprout header, in a row of much older ladies, veteran hands at this work stand. Seven ladies stood at a pile of green sprouts needing to get their untidy heads trimmed by a machine cutter; very tedious task all day and noisy too. Rudi was filling boxes, heaving full crates everywhere and sweeping-up along the line trying to block-out the noise. Everything else he did like: all the people at honest toil, real work in big sheds and good pay. It was Rudi's idea of education, his rites of passage for western manhood. He knew the other men thought the same, specially the younger men. His foreman was not so young, but forceful and fair; taking a steady look at each man as he instructed them; following up with a straight walk and flat voice across the shoulders directly into the ear. "Stop talking to these women, you got that", he told Rudi. When Rudi tried to respond the foreman stared longer, directly at his nose. So he just turned away, as if to obey, if he could remember.

The next work break found Rudi in quiet repose and alone --

"Can you help me with my overall, fix the straps please"?

"Alright, turn around".

"My name is Rosa and thanks".

But letting his hands upon her was not really okay, because she was young and vital and Rudi naturally shy. Soon as he touched her she spoke more about the job and how they could work together. Next day he had to hear more about a boyfriend, money trouble and her father. It was a full bio, a jumbled story without ready answers and put out for serious purpose which made Rudi nervous; because she was young but not innocent, attractive but not free.

There was only one way out the cannery to the parking lot, where employees gathered to smoke or chat and the other way to a canteen upstairs. So Rudi could not hope to avoid Rosa, could not steer away from trouble like this easily, he had to ride hard through it.

"Hey there, are you going any better? D'you like the place yet; you will soon; as we all do". Rudi took a bold initiative one day and blew out a smoke screen towards her. "This is the 'produce state' for all our America. Heck, our 'GNP' here is greater than most foreign countries" he said "and us also part of the denim culture, so we all swim in the same stream; okay, good. Great to see the gals dig this; why not"! He surprised himself, with this kind of talk he made-up, hoping it would work --

"Hey, that's really far-out, yeah"! She grinned and relaxed; seemed to comprehend the flattery and enjoy some pride, before they went off upstairs. They shared a big dish of pasta, old style, with thick meat lumps and dull red sauce. Rosa ate steadily while talking and Rudi playing his part in a Cannery Row like drama; thinking of John Steinbeck's characters in Monterey. In 'Cannery Row' and 'Tortilla Flat' sardines and fish were taken from the sea; here in San Cutraz it was sprouts from the fields up the coast. One big area of flat green fields were cut every morning, trucked to the site, then boxed and frozen by the same evening. It was heroic work, with men and women together, making a good clean food product.

Rudi drove the coast route one weekend, to find these fields; a fine time to see everything from his big sedan. There was no traffic and no difficulty; a straight road north with just two lanes of blacktop: one side were the fields, the other side was the famed Pacific Ocean. Stretching all the way from San Cutraz to San Francisco, the water seemed tame that day, no stormy waves and no whitecaps; a big disappointment the way an ocean only licked the shoreline and melted away to the horizon in a very ordinary sea-blue colour. He passed some cafes and roadside stop-overs, but was not diverted and kept a steady speed with radio humming; his left arm crooked out the open window so he could feel the journey, feel the miles he covered. Men in the old days rode long trails in the West that same way, savouring the sight of mountains and forests; following the rushing streams and camping in the clear meadows. Travelling was a big American thing; what they did best and what they all did. Well heck, travelling got the country started; even now men still journeyed every day for one reason or another – it was American as hot apple pie.

Rudi went up to San Francisco to see his friends, for a city point-of-view, a faster pace. Meanwhile his old sedan followed the road alongside the blue ocean for a hundred miles, on a clear September day; to see how the sprouts grew across open level spaces, big square patches of green, small round sprouts on a small leafy bush. They were cultivated by California farmers on a grand scale, not like garden produce; more romantic with the largesse, the whole benefit and the plant growing part. The sun shone at its best, showing the green growth as yellowing gold, when radiant beams fell across the field onto the row lines. Rudi recalled the famed grape vines he saw in Sonoma and Napa; the same long rows of tidy green plants, between strips of clean brown earth.

He tried to tell his city pals how he had gone through open farmland that morning, the same crop to cut for his cannery, the same fields to be harvested for their sprouts. But he went to meet-up with lawyers, a teacher and librarian; what would they care of Rudi's concerns, except as amusing and distracting. Rudi sought them out in a way they did not really need, because they never went out of the

141

city. Sadly, it was a one-sided contact, which continued unchanged for years. They did not even want to know about a young girl like Rosa, or the archetypal foreman.

The next night, after a long shift at work, Rudi went across town to eat; somewhere new, because his wage was good and promising. It was a premier steak house, where he parked his vehicle at one side, then marched inside in his work duds. But he was welcomed fairly and seated easily at the center. He decided on ribs and coffee. Later he would not remember the food, but did remember the coffee, the many refills. He seemed to be thirsty that night and specially needing strong drink, like coffee was just invented, or him returned from a long odyssey. The other diners were at end of their evening, winding down with drinks and slumping in the soft seats, too tired to notice a real stranger in their midst. Rudi noticed them and how he was out of place in a family eatery; needing to wash and shave and needing table friends. But he tried to think things through at his place; like the weekend just past, what he did and what his pals might say amongst themselves; to understand something new on his drive back at night. Though nothing would come to him from this crowd; they too were well out of reach, sufficiently distant. Nothing came to him to change a basic sense of food after work, a sense of his own instinct raw and undirected. Mostly he felt free like a beast upon the hills, hungry and restless. Was he enjoying this kind of freedom, or was it only ignorance, he finally muttered into his last napkin? He went off home feeling unsettled for sleep – food and drink was never enough, even if it was good, something was missing.

The following weekend Rudi wanted to visit his regular café-bar and not sit with noisy strangers. But no chance, because he forgot about his gamey neighbour, another misfit on the block. Jack was not a lawyer or teacher, not even finishing up school; but needed to seek out Rudi to go across town with him.

"Hey, Rudi, down here"!

A car horn sounded loudly at the street corner, from a large ugly Buick at the curb; so knew it had to be Jack and could not be ignored.

The car was old and dusty, a big family saloon, except Jack never had a family; but he had Rudi now and was ready to eat somewhere by seven o'clock. Jack was not old or dusty; he was forty-something, with five o'clock shadow and spreading middle; very much regretting his younger days in Los Angeles, the way he told it. He was angry and bitter about his mis-spent youth which seemed to somehow reflect on Rudi. But there was some kindness in him and interest in the plight of another young man new to San Cutraz County.

"Let's go, sport, hold on" – Jack roared up the engine and steered down Beach Road to go right, then along the ocean to a river inlet; where a nice lounge diner appeared on the bank side. It was lively and spacious, offering harbour views for some of the tables outside on a patio near to the water. There were a lot of deep couches and leather seating in an open area, where the mood was comfortable and restful; as if the customers were all bad tempered bears or hungry bears. It had the right effect upon Rudi straight away and Jack went smartly inside like he wanted to own the place. Yet he looked tired and worn in his frayed shirt with seven o'clock stubble, so obvious to Rudi and the waiter; possibly worrying for patrons at the next table. After a few minutes nothing happened, no one said anything, so Rudi could unwind and think of things to order. It was like this each week, at a different place; lots of awkward moments and rough jokes over the table, spilling water and crumbs across the white linen. Bread was always first for Rudi, warm sweet rolls from the kitchen oven, butter and first taste of wine --

"Nothing's changed, squire".

"What's that"?

"About bringing home the bacon and about excitement. Comfort is what you want and lasts longer than excitement". Jack said all this a hundred times, but tried to make it sound new; he felt important with Rudi, the way he listened and learned. This was meant to be Jack's night, his show. Though his table talk and horse sense were very stale, his intros for Rudi were expansive and welcome; the way he was free with money and how he wanted Rudi to sample the best kind of eating place.

Next day they rode together in the Buick again, to drive out further towards Salinas and the county fair; a nice straight ride to a big show ground. Jack was still not shaved and trying to continue his dialogue from last night; a sort of polemic for younger men, together with personal confessions. Rudi took no notice today; he was out in old Americana he knew from home and taking in the bigger picture.

"Those gals love their ponies, while Daddy's still paying".

"Which one you admiring, Jack"?

"Any which way you can see, squire".

They were watching the barrel racing, run in age groups, sitting on wooden boarding behind the arena fence. The young girls wore boy's gear: denim pants and stud shirts, with a big dark Stetson covering braided hair. Their backsides banged hard into the saddle when they stretched forward over the reins; proud gals and handsome with it. A 'Mariachi' band could be heard playing further away, yet it was clear and effective; making for a bright mood everywhere and the sun shone gently, was friendly. Rudi suddenly thought about Rosa, if she would like to ride, if she ever had a pony. He could ask her next session at the cannery, back at their work place; when he had to find something to say, something to talk about. Jack said he only liked facts and things he could see/hold onto infront of him; was a practical man he said and set to instruct Rudi. But the two of them spent enough time together to confirm respect and enjoyment; respect across the generations and enjoyment of outdoor pursuits they both knew from before. All this played out evenly while watching the show animals, shouting at events or wandering the grounds. Returning to San Cutraz, their vehicle went directly into the setting sun, which had its own nostalgia and its own quiet end. Getting back to the curb outside Rudi's place, Jack left quickly, like a bad spell came upon them and Rudi was nervous about rising early next morning.

By season end Rudi had to find fresh work, when the fields were all cut with no sprouts left to gather. He had to seek elsewhere for a job; another work situation fit for a young man with an open mind and honest need for wages. It did not take long, as this was a small town and word-of-mouth went round quickly.

A good clean and well lighted place, the other side of town; a new place opening all hours all week, was enough for Rudi to get hired at night. It was a lonely shift at this garage, but peaceful and quiet enough to write letters home. After one or two customers came in very late for a tank of gas or quick service, he set to clean the site top-to-bottom. He enjoyed blasting two washrooms with the water hose, for a quick once-over, aiming the water spray over the walls, floor, like he was at a riot. He went on to sweep the lot, picking up everything from cigarette ends to shreds of litter, far out as the street. He also cleared the tools from work benches to tidy away, then got out his pen and paper.

Last thing one night Rudi was quietly alone; some unknown people came into the station before he could get out the hosepipe. They drove a small VW auto to the pumps and a young woman was in the rear lowering down the window to talk –

"Hi, what you doing, what happened to you" she said?

Her friends were tired and grumpy, "Shut up girl, sit back in there", someone answered; which was enough to stop her.

"Okay, bye". It was the girl from the cannery, the Asian girl, showing up at Rudi's work place again.

"Hi! How is your baby" Rudi said? "Yeah, I'm good". He saw her briefly, then only dark shapes at the window. When the engine re-started Rudi stepped aside in-line with the pump stand.

"Here, ten dollars – thanks – goodnight"! A young man was in the driving seat and moved off forcefully. He would not look at Rudi; he was looking seriously ahead into the depth of night, into the dark unknown.

He noticed freckles upon her face, across her nose and a clear sense she was glad to see him, a big surprise at this hour. At the same time Rudi realized how it was awkward and might lead to trouble; when the husband was there in charge and with his friends. Of course he missed her; they spent a lot of time together before and working at a new place did not change anything for them. Making friends with any gal was never a simple affair; a lot of other people were always involved, rightly or wrongly. It was not easy to contract a fair and equitable friendship with anyone unless a lot of things were understood, if it was to be short-lived, or somehow held a secret.

AFTERWORD/AUTHOR

There is a 'Vedder River' in Canada (BC), which flows from Chilliwack Lake into the mighty Fraser River. It is a strong flowing river, full of salmon returning in the season, with masses of tree cover and small settlements/claims hidden from view. Vedder Road goes south from town and crosses a narrow reach of the river, then onto another lake beyond. This old service road now also crosses two new tracks going in very different directions; one way is back up into the mountains towards isolated cabins, fishing lodges and work sites. This country is largely unspoiled and little known, always a surprise/pleasure to find.

* * *

I began life in the UK (Northeast); with ships and shipyards providing employment for my family, from generations back. A dramatic change after school, took me into farming in Yorkshire/Northumberland, where I met different kinds of working people. Later I was lucky enough to attend the RAC in Gloucestershire; a residential college for young men, in lovely farming country, with small market town at hand. But in my second year, it became apparent that farming was not likely to be a satisfactory career for me. I began reading seriously and thinking of Canada/America, after my father relocated to British Columbia. I purchased a first edition of 'A Moveable Feast' by Hemingway and was enthralled; reading the book in my bedroom and neglecting my farm classes. Upon leaving college I was thinking of a different career; except the rural spirit got into my system by then and directed my interests/work and travel for the next ten years. Poetry was my first serious writing, fiction not attempted until years later in London, where I began a first story (Bicycle Friends) after a solid period of teaching in schools.

Teaching still interests me, enough to continue private tuition and creating new lesson materials. After joining 'Mensa-UK' in 1997, I also enjoyed writing short articles on current affairs and travel. Friends say I am very British (not denied); though I still yearn for the big spaces in America, the open road, new kinds of people (native Indians) and compelling landscapes. A lot of poetry has been written before finishing this book, which turned out to be good preparation for me; because the westcoast is romantic, rueful and pastoral; full of wonderful imagery, scenes of colour and feeling, people of meaning and interest.

I was secondary teacher with English Literature/Language; mostly in London/UK after college in Canada (SFU). And still in-touch with old friends in California... dreaming of long road trips to Wyoming or Utah and such like, across the 'great divide' into the 'high chaparral'; encountering all before me in my own sweet time... staying in ole-style motels, eating in forgotten diners and talking to strangers --

Lightning Source UK Ltd.
Milton Keynes UK
UKOW06f2159170415

249857UK00001B/17/P